The Easy

Wildflower

Guide

The Easy

Wildflower
Guide

Written and Photographed
by Neil Fletcher

Paintings by Gill Tomblin

First published in Great Britain by Aurum Press Ltd
25 Bedford Avenue, London WC1B 3AT

© Duncan Petersen Publishing Ltd 2005

© Text and pictures, Neil Fletcher

A catalogue record of this book is available from the British Library

ISBN 1-84513-039-1

Printed in Thailand by Imago

Conceived, edited, designed and produced by Duncan Petersen Publishing, 31 Ceylon Road,
London W14 0PY

Editor Sophie Page
Designers Tony Chung and Ian Midson
Editorial Director Andrew Duncan

Acknowledgements for photos: Ted Benton for Wood Sorrel; Late Spider Orchid; Nils Sloth
for Meadow Saxifrage; Mike Read for Grass of Parnassus; Cowberry

Foreword

Fascinated by all forms of wildlife, it was before my teenage years that I first looked at the wild flowers growing on a nearby patch of wasteland and wanted to put a name to them.

On opening one of the few field guides available I was immediately beset by over a thousand plants to choose from, all in scientific 'taxonomic' order – there was no clue where to start. Even having narrowed it down by laboriously examining all the tiny illustrations, the descriptions were full of jargon and botanical nomenclature; I felt I'd have to become a qualified scientist before I could even understand the book.

Considerable time has passed since then and as my expertise has grown I've realised that identifying wild flowers, just as identifying birds, is not about the fine details of every petal, (or every feather), but relies on the general impression and appearance of the whole plant, so that as one gets to know them they may be instantly recognized, almost as friends, even when speeding past a colourful embankment on the motorway.

Sadly, many wild flower guides are still produced with a bewildering array of species, complicated keys and technical language, all of which only serve to discourage the beginner from moving beyond the first hurdle of identification. With this *Easy Guide* I have tried to remove those hurdles, making wild flower recognition the rewarding experience which it should be, and encouraging the reader to understand more about the fascinating world of nature that surrounds us.

Neil Fletcher
Spring 2005

Field Forget-me-not

Contents

About this book

CAN A WILDFLOWER GUIDE REALLY BE EASY?

Yes provided that the key facts – those that point to the right name for the plant – are presented in a clear and self-evident way. In this guide we make an unusually clear distinction between the overall appearance of a wild flower (in the photo on the right hand page) and the fine details that pin down identification (in the artwork panel on the left hand page).

HOW EASY?

In making this the easy wildflower guide, we have concentrated on several key points:

● **A manageable number of species, carefully selected.** There are more than 2,500 species of wild flower in northwestern Europe (and more than 10,000 if one includes the distinctive habitats of the Mediterranean region), which represents a bewildering number of choices, especially to the novice. The great majority of these flowers are no more than slightly differing variations of a group of species which are essentially very similar, whilst many others are either extremely rare or only found in remote locations. The 232 species covered in detail in this book have been carefully selected to represent those that you are most likely to want to identify. Most of them are common and eye-catching. A few are less striking, but so common that they cannot be ignored. Some are less common, but so conspicuous as to demand attention.

● **Simple language.** The text is free of jargon and technical terms, and explains simply the key features to look out for on the plant, as well as its general appearance when seen growing in the wild. Most people don't carry a tape measure with them on a country walk, and so the size of the plant is described in terms of the human body – knee-height, chest-height, ankle-height and so on.

Tormentil

Meadow Buttercup

Field Forget-me-not

● **Similar-looking flowers are grouped together.** Many books, indeed most books, group flowers together in taxonomic order – a system used by scientists based on the reproductive parts of the flower, with the most primitive such as nettles at the beginning and most complex such as orchids at the end. This makes it almost impossible to find a plant quickly unless you know to which family the plant belongs, and where that family appears in the taxonomic order.

● *The Easy Wildflower Guide* groups all plants with the same flower colour together. Within each colour group, those with the same general appearance appear close to each other, so that Tormentil (shown left) is placed close to Meadow Buttercup (shown left), for instance. These are two unrelated species, but they nonetheless look similar and grow in the same situations.

● **Crystal-clear photographs and paintings of each species.** Compared to other mammals, human beings have a very highly developed sense of sight, with particularly good colour vision. We are visual animals that use our eyesight above all other senses to understand the world around us.

It is the visual appearance of wild flowers that gives us our first impression of them, and so this book uses large, clear photographs and we present them in an uncluttered way. Most of the photos were taken especially for this book. They show the most obvious and striking features of the plant, growing wild in its natural habitat.

In addition, specially-commissioned artwork illustrates the most important parts in close-up, such as leaves, flowers and fruits.

● **Information you will remember.** In many cases the text includes fascinating information about the plant: perhaps how it has been used as a medical treatment or as a food source; a particularly interesting point about its biology, or some folklore. Having identified a forget-me-not (shown above) for the first time, you may not remember that it has 10 mm flowers with five rounded petals and spear-shaped leaves, but you may well remember the tale of the knight who tossed a posy of the flowers to his lover on the river-bank, as he sank into the depths of the swirling waters.

What is a flower?

In the true sense of the word, a flower is the reproductive organ, or a collection of organs, of a plant. The term is used much more generally however to mean the plants themselves.

It is easy to forget, therefore, that almost all plants possess flowers: trees, grasses, even those plants which we regard as 'weeds' all have flowers. Those plants which genuinely do not possess flowers are the more primitive or insignificant kinds, such as mosses, ferns or lichens.

Wild flowers hold an important place in our imaginations. They engage our senses with their bright colours; their delightful perfumes, or offensive odours; their simple, basic patterns or complex sculptural forms; their soft, downy leaves or their aggressive thorns.

In this book, we take a 'wild flower' to mean any plant that occurs naturally in the countryside, including some that were originally grown only in gardens but have since developed wild populations of their own. In common with other flower books, we have not included trees or grasses. A few plants are included which could be described as shrubs. These have been chosen because of their impressive and colourful blooms, such as Dog Rose and Gorse (both shown below).

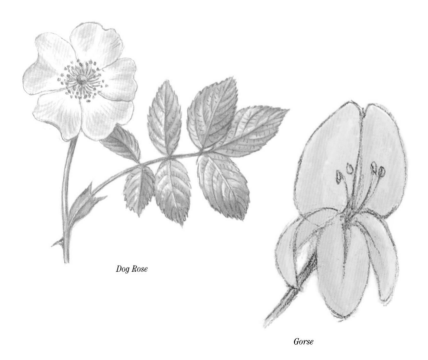

Dog Rose

Gorse

The status of wild flowers

Gorse

Until two centuries ago, more than 80 per cent of the population of Europe lived outside cities in small towns, villages or in completely rural situations in the heart of the countryside. Living with wildlife, including flowers, was a part of everyday existence.

None of the basic products that we take for granted today were then available, such as simple medicines, antiseptics, deodorants and so on. There were no supermarkets importing foodstuffs from around the globe, and without mechanical transport, perishable goods could only be sourced locally, except for the very wealthy.

As a result, the wild flowers and other plants of the countryside were viewed as a vast and wonderful resource – for food, and for household remedies. The names of the flowers that grew locally would have been familiar to almost everyone. Indeed, the accurate identification of plants was an essential part of a child's education, as many of them are mildly poisonous, and a few fatally so.

However, during the 19th and 20th centuries, the rise of industry and the migration to cities meant that many people, except for farmers, lost touch with nature on a day-to-day basis. There were enormous advances in science too, and coupled with modernist principles, the 'old ways' of herbal remedies became regarded as superstitious folklore.

In recent decades, however, an increasing number of people have started once more to appreciate the healing properties of plants, either as a natural alternative, or to complement modern medicines, and there is a greater awareness of the environment.

We are more sensitive than ever to the fragility of the natural world and how easily it may be destroyed, and there are a growing number of people wishing to get back in touch with nature. So, wild flowers are enjoying something of a revival and they are all the more interesting because they are excellent indicators of the health of the environment.

How to use this book

TAKE THE BOOK TO THE PLANT

It is all too easy to think that you will be able to remember the details of some brightly-coloured or imposing plant seen in a hedgerow while out on a country walk. On returning home and consulting the book hours afterwards, it's a different story: were the leaves really lobed like that? Were there five petals or six? Not only are you unsure, but your memory is fading.

CHOOSE THE APPROPRIATE COLOUR SECTION

The book has been divided into eight colour sections representing the dominant colour of the flower in question. The first section covers white and white-to-pink flowers: many plants have white flowers which are flushed with a pink tinge, and some produce flowers of either colour. Then follow flowers which are always a more or less deep pink; then red flowers and so on, following the order of colours in the rainbow, ending with purple.

Of course there have to be exceptions to this apparently neat system. Nature is not so easily reduced to order. You need to know that a few plants produce flowers in a range of colours on separate plants. Common Comfrey (shown below) produces flowers in creamy-white, pink or violet-blue, Common Milkwort (shown below) has flowers which are usually blue, but may be pink or white, and the purple flowers of Honesty (shown below) and Sweet Violet are sometimes produced in white.

However, all of these colour variations can usually be found growing close together, and it is the most commonly seen that determines into which colour section of the book the plant has been placed. Although both Common and Heath Spotted Orchids (shown right) produce white as well as pink flowers, they have been placed with the other orchids in the pink section so that comparison is that much easier.

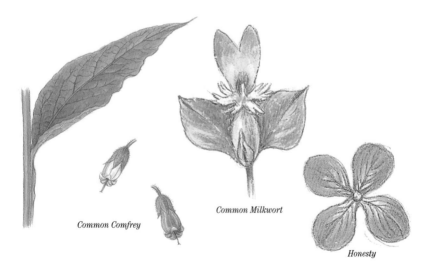

Common Milkwort

Common Comfrey

Honesty

12

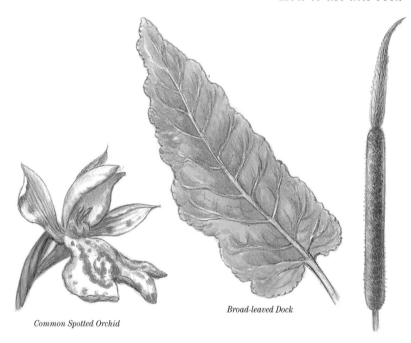

Common Spotted Orchid

Broad-leaved Dock

Bulrush

The green section of the book includes those plants which produce often rather insignificant green flowers, though some may start out green and change colour as the fruits develop, for example to red in the case of Broad-leaved Dock (shown above), or brown in the case of Bulrush (shown above).

Once you are sure that you are in the right colour section, leaf through its pages. Plants with a similar general appearance are grouped like with like.

CHECK THE DETAILS AGAINST THE ILLUSTRATIONS

The paintings show close-up views of the leaves, flowers, and sometimes the fruits so that identification can be confirmed. Annotations give a clear indication of particular points to look out for.

OTHER CLUES TO CHECK

●**Habitat.** A habitat 'key' painting in the main text gives an instant guide to where the plant usually grows. This is backed up by further description within the text. Many plants are very particular about such factors as soil conditions, moisture or the amount of light available, and these are often excellent clues to correct identification.

●**Range.** A map of Europe at the bottom of the right-hand page for each species shows the general area where the plant occurs. Note that the right habitat must still be present in that area. For example: Bogbean (page 60) has a range that

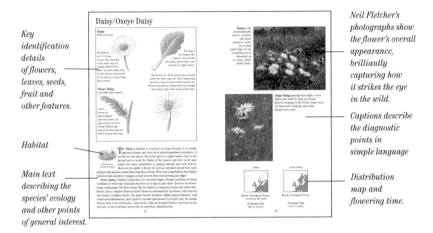

Key identification details of flowers, leaves, seeds, fruit and other features.

Habitat

Main text describing the species' ecology and other points of general interest.

Neil Fletcher's photographs show the flower's overall appearance, brilliantly capturing how it strikes the eye in the wild.

Captions describe the diagnostic points in simple language

Distribution map and flowering time.

covers almost all of Europe, but will only be found where there are acidic bog habitats. Very occasionally, a plant may be found growing outside its usual range, but these rarely form permanent populations.

● **Flowering period.** An indication is given (below the map) of the times of year during which the plant may produce flowers. Some plants continue to flower continuously throughout this period, while others may produce a 'flush' of flowers at the beginning, but then flower sporadically for a few weeks or months if conditions allow. Note that flowering time is often much earlier in southern Europe than in the north, and the flowering period stated reflects the whole range of possible flowering times.

● **Growing height.** The height to which a plant grows is governed, within limits, by conditions such as soil fertility and moisture, competition with other plants and how much light there is. For example, Red Clover will grow much taller in long grass in order to expose its leaves to the sky. There is, however, a range within which any species will usually grow, and this is indicated by a comparison to the average human body – knee-height, chest-height and so on. Note that in some cases, plants may grow much shorter than is usual, especially if it has been grazed or mown down earlier, or where the climate is particularly harsh.

● **Similar species.** In many cases, the text briefly describes other species similar to the one illustrated. All those species covered by the book have been carefully selected to represent the major groups of plants, so it should still be possible to identify to which group an unidentified plant belongs. For example, there are 20 or so speedwells (*Veronica* species) in northeastern Europe, but they all have the same flower-shape and general appearance as those covered by this book.

Where flowers grow

All plants have specific requirements about where they will grow: their preferred habitat. Some are more adaptable than others, and may be found in a greater range of conditions, but even in these cases there will be a common link, such as the soil type. The main environmental factors affecting plants are as follows:

● **Sun or shade.** All flowering plants need light in order to manufacture food, though there are a few exceptions, for example, the saprophytic plants that feed on decaying matter in the soil, which they do with the help of fungi. Generally speaking, though, the more light there is, the better a plant can perform photosynthesis, the chemical reaction that takes place when the leaves are exposed to sunlight, forming sugar within the cells which the plant uses as food. Some plants are better adapted to shady conditions than others, and this has advantages: there is often less competition with other plants for nutrients in the soil, and the humid atmosphere reduces the risk of drying out. However, growth in a shady situation takes place more slowly than in a sunny one, and even moderately shade-loving plants such as Nipplewort (shown right) and Orpine do not reach their full flowering maturity until well into the summer.

Nipplewort

If you look carefully at how the leaves are arranged on the stems of plants, you can see how they avoid casting shade over each other: they are placed at alternate right-angles, or spirally up the stem but decreasing in size, or in whorls which do not quite overlap.

● **Wet or dry.** Plants that grow in permanently wet situations have an obvious advantage: they do not have to struggle in order to find enough water. However, there is often great competition for growing space in these areas – compare the lush growth on a riverbank to the sparse vegetation of a dry shingle beach. In some cases, plants are adapted to dealing with the limited space available in the margins of shallow water by growing very tall and very thin leaves, as in Flowering Rush (shown right) and Yellow Flag. Plants living in dry conditions face less competition, but inevitably grow smaller and more slowly, and in very arid situations are adapted to conserve moisture within their leaves, such as Biting Stonecrop.

Flowering Rush

● **Acid or alkaline.** The acidity or alkalinity of the soil pH has a considerable bearing on which species of plants will grow because it affects the amount of soil nutrients which are available for the plant. Alkaline or basic soils normally occur over a chalk or limestone bedrock, and provide good growing conditions for a very wide range of plants: many orchids grow on chalky soils, for instance, as do herbs such as Wild Thyme (shown right) and Wild Marjoram. Strongly acidic soils, by contrast, such as those on heaths and bogs, support only a small range of plants, though they may occur in large quantities, as do Heather and Bogbean. There is, of course, a continuous spectrum of soil pH between very acid and very alkaline (soils midway between the two are called neutral soils), but there are only a few plants, such as Bulrush, which can tolerate the full range: most are quite specific in their requirements.

Wild Thyme

● **Rich or poor.** Some plants require very rich, fertile soils and it is often these that we regard as farmland weeds such as Mugwort (shown right) and Curled Dock. They thrive where nitrogen-rich fertilizers have been added to the soil, growing quickly and forming large colonies, blocking out the light at ground level so that little else can grow. Paradoxically, poorer soils support a much wider diversity of plants, as each individual plant is unable to grow strongly enough to out-compete its neighbour. So on thin soils over chalk, for instance, there may be as many as 30 or more species of flowering plant in one square metre. The very poorest soils however, on mountain tops or on walls, may have bare patches devoid of any plants at all.

Mugwort

● **Disturbed or established** soils that have been ploughed, dug up, driven over or otherwise disturbed provide a useful habitat for pioneer species – plants which require bare ground to begin a new colony. Also most annuals (those that reproduce every year from seed), require disturbed soils for the seeds to germinate without competition from other plants. These plants are particularly common in man-made habitats: without man's intervention, disturbed ground would only occur where a natural trauma had occurred, such as a violent storm or flood, or where heavy grazing animals have 'poached' the soil with their hooves. Established soils allow perennial plants to set up permanent colonies, and sometimes soil fungi are present which contribute to the success of certain plants. Woodland is an extreme example of vegetation on established soil, but old meadows and even pastures may have established vegetation if they have been managed the same way for centuries.

Conservation

WHY ARE SOME FLOWERS RARE?

Some flowers can reproduce more easily and live in a wider variety of conditions than others. Dandelion (shown right) is an example of one such highly successful plant. Others have more specific requirements of their habitat, and if these conditions become less frequent, then the plant is unable to survive. Without doubt, habitat loss is the most important conservation issue that faces plants, and wild animals too, for that matter. There are two major causes of habitat destruction:

Dandelion

●**Development.** Increasingly large areas of land are being taken over for housing and industry. Obviously this has a direct impact on the habitat. Not so obvious is development's much wider effect. The demand for water by increased urbanization has led to the drainage of marshes and other wetlands, lowering the underground water table and water levels in rivers. At the same time, inland reservoirs created by flooding valleys cover vast areas and make relatively poor habitats for wildlife. Road building carves the land into fragments, so that populations of plants become separated, with small populations being unable to sustain themselves.

●**Modern farming practices.** Ancient forms of farming were very beneficial to wildlife and actually led to an increased diversity of habitats, but modern intensive grazing (for example) means that fields have to be artificially fertilized. This meant that pastures support only a few species of grass and are almost devoid of flowers. Fertilizers and herbicides, used on arable fields, mean that only monocultures of crops exist which at one time would have had a rich and colourful flora of 'weed' species intermingled with the crop, which in turn provided food for insects and birds. However, species-rich fields can still be seen, notably on areas that are farmed organically. Many old woodlands have been cut down, only to be replaced with intensive ranks of fast-growing conifers, which shut out the light completely and acidify the soil, impoverishing it even further.

Those areas of land which have not been degraded are becoming smaller and smaller, and further and further apart from each other. So it becomes increasingly less likely that pollen, or ripe seed, will find its way from where the parent plant is growing to another fragment of suitable habitat, which may be kilometres away. This means that some plants, especially the less adaptable ones, are vulnerable to extinction from a local area of suitable habitat: if they disappear from there, they have no hope of return. For this reason, some species are protected from picking by law, though which species varies from country to country. The legal situation is too complex to summarize and our simple request to readers of this guide is not to pick flowers from the wild at all. And of course, never dig them up, as that removes them completely.

TECHNICAL TERMS

Wherever possible, the use of technical terms and jargon have been kept to a minimum throughout the book, and in many instances less familiar terms have been explained in context where they have been used. Nevertheless, the study of plants necessarily involves some words and phrases that require further explanation, a few of which are defined here.

Words that appear in italics are defined elsewhere in the glossary.

Anther: the upper, club-like part of the stamen which contains the pollen grains.

Axil: the angle between two structures, such as the leaf-stalk and the main stem.

Bract: a structure at the base of the flower-stalk, often appearing very similar to a leaf, though not always so. In daisy-type flowers, for instance, the bracts form a cup of narrow green strips that support the tiny florets, and in *umbelliferous* flowers they are usually very slender segments at the hub of the 'wheel' of flower-stalks.

Bracteole: like a bract on *umbelliferous* flowers, but formed closer to the flowers, at the base of the smaller branches.

Bulbil: a small, bulb-like organ that breaks off to form a new plant. They may be clustered among the flowers, in the axils of leaves, or at the base of the plant.

Chalky soil: in this guide the term has been used to describe any soil which lies over a chalk or limestone bedrock, and is therefore alkaline in its nature.

Character: a feature of a plant that helps to distinguish it from others, for example the two lines of hairs on

the stems of Germander Speedwell, or the column-like *style* on the flowers of Field Rose.

Disc floret: in the daisy family, a flower in the central part of the flower-head, whose petals are fused into a tiny tube.

Disturbed ground: land that is frequently or occasionally cultivated or dug over such as farmland, gardens and road verges, and providing habitat particularly for *pioneer species*.

Escape: a plant often cultivated in gardens or as a crop, but which has become established in the wild.

Family: a formal term for a group of plants with similar characteristics, containing one or more closely related *genera*.

Floret: one of a group of small, individual flowers clustered together to form a flower-head.

Genus (plural, Genera): a formal term grouping together one or more closely related species. The genus is the first part of the two-word scientific or Latin name of a plant, and is always written with its initial letter in upper case, e.g. *Veronica chamaedrys*; *Veronica persica*, so both of these species belong to the genus *Veronica*.

Habitat: the preferred home of a plant, where a set of required conditions are met such as soil type; amount of light; moisture and so on.

Lip: a protruding petal as in members of the Orchid and Mint families.

Ovary: the female part of the flower that contains the undeveloped seeds, usually found at the base of the petals, though sometimes found below them.

Pioneer species: a plant that is one of the first to colonize bare ground.

Pollen: the tiny dust-like grains produced by the flower which provide the male cells necessary for reproduction – just as in the sperm of animals.

Pollination: the successful placement of *pollen* upon the female parts (*stigma*) of a flower, often performed by insects, though many plants are wind-pollinated.

Ray floret: in the daisy family, a flower with a single, ribbon-like petal, usually in the outer part of the flower-head though dandelion-type flower-heads are composed entirely of ray florets.

Rhizome: a thickened stem (usually underground) which serves as a food storage organ.

Runner: a stem which creeps along the ground, forming roots at intervals and eventually new plants.

Sepal: a structure that surrounds the petals when the flower is in bud, though they vary greatly in size and shape. When the flower has no true petals they are sometimes brightly coloured and perform the same role as the petals themselves. All the sepals together are collectively known as the calyx.

Stamen: the male organ of a flower, with a thin stalk called a filament holding up the *anther*.

Stigma: the female part of the flower that receives the *pollen*.

Stipule: a leaf-like structure at the base of the leaf-stalk.

Style: the female part of the flower that joins the *ovary* to the *stigma*, often shaped like a narrow tube.

Species: a formal term defining a group of similar individuals that breed true in the wild. The species is indicated by the second part of the two-word scientific or Latin name of a plant, and is always written entirely in lower case, e.g. *Veronica chamaedrys* is a species of the genus *Veronica*.

Spur: a hollow tube or pouch projecting from the back of a flower, usually containing nectar and which can only be reached by long-tongued insects (these are larger and therefore more effective pollinators).

Trifoliate: describes a leaf made up of three distinct leaflets, for instance the clovers.

Tuber: a swollen underground organ formed from the stem or roots that stores food for the plant, so that it may grow quickly after a dormant period – usually the winter.

Umbellifer: a member of the carrot family, whose flowers form a domed or flat cluster on stalks which are arranged like the spokes of a wheel – called an umbel.

Habitat keys

Woodland – the canopy of trees provides shelter to plants from the drying effects of wind and strong summer sunlight. The shade produced, however, may be too dark for many plants, and so woodland edges or glades and clearings within the wood are often the best places to look. Dense hedgerows provide a similar effect. The soil in woodlands is rich in nutrients, though coniferous woodlands have an acidic soil due to the rotting pine needles and a much lower plant diversity.

Hedgerows and roadsides – hedges of shrubs or small trees provide a platform for climbing plants, and shelter from the wind whilst allowing plenty of sunlight to reach the ground. The soil next to roads and tracks is subject to disturbance from wheeled and foot traffic, and to regular maintenance by mowing, and so provides a combination of several other habitat aspects together. They may be very rich in different types of plants.

Grassy meadows – areas of grassland may become established over centuries, provided that they continue to be managed as such, either by grazing or mowing for hay, and can be very rich in flowers. Plants may be adapted to deal with this regular cutting down by forming leafy rosettes close to the ground, or growing and flowering quickly in the short season available. Such areas often have very good drainage and frequently occur on slopes, with slight shelter provided by scattered bushes or scrub.

Rough wasteland – derelict sites close to buildings or farms provide disturbed soils, often rather dry and low in nutrients, and are ideal for many pioneer plants and annuals that require bare soil to establish themselves. Such places may have few grasses present, but a range of flowering plants that grow quickly to form colonies in the absence of competition from other plants.

Farmland – arable fields provide a combination of regularly disturbed soils and very high nutrient levels as a result of artificial fertilizers, and provide the perfect home for many annual species. However, the use of herbicides may mean that wild flowers are confined to the very edges of such fields. 'Improved' pastures – permanent grassland with fertilizers added – is often very poor in wild flowers as they cannot compete with the robust growth of the grasses.

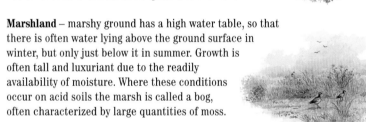

Heathland – acidic, sandy soils may be dominated by a low shrubby layer of Heather intermixed with just a few other specialized species that can cope with the acid conditions, with wetter areas where the drainage is poor generally providing the places of greatest plant diversity. Most plants are usually short due to the low nutrient levels available and exposure to the wind.

Marshland – marshy ground has a high water table, so that there is often water lying above the ground surface in winter, but only just below it in summer. Growth is often tall and luxuriant due to the readily availability of moisture. Where these conditions occur on acid soils the marsh is called a bog, often characterized by large quantities of moss.

Ponds and ditches – open water habitats are suitable for truly aquatic plants that require their roots to be completely covered with water at all times. Although they are open to the full sun there is no danger of drying out, and their shape or 'growth habit' varies greatly depending on the depth of water in which they grow, so they may have leaves which float on the water surface, or leaves which are tall, narrow and erect where the water is shallower.

Coast – the land close to the sea receives the full force of the wind and sun, and has very little fresh water available, either because the soils are well drained or because the water is salty. Plants growing here are usually low to the ground and are adapted in various ways to avoid desiccation, often with rather succulent leaves.

Hedge Bindweed / Field Bindweed

Hedge Bindweed
Calystegia sepium

Field Bindweed
Convolvulus arvensis

Bright green leaves are arranged alternately on the thin, twining stems, broadly arrow-shaped and often somewhat glossy on the upper surface, especially when young.

Leaves may be narrow and strongly arrow-shaped, or oval with the slightest suggestion of arrow 'tails', and are often a dark, dull green.

The white trumpet-shaped flowers are 30-50 mm across, with two bracts at the base, not quite overlapping, which surround the sepals. Large Bindweed (*Calystegia sylvatica*) has even larger flowers, with bracts that completely overlap each other.

Flowers are 20-30 mm across, sometimes white but more often pink with white stripes. The sepals are not covered by large bracts. The flowers close up in dull weather.

Hedgerows, roadsides

Hedge Bindweed produces an abundance of beautiful pure white flowers in late summer; it's seen typically in hedgerows, on wasteground and climbing fences. Were it not such a pernicious weed of gardens, it would undoubtedly earn greater respect. The thin, wiry roots are extremely difficult to eradicate from the soil, and the tough stems twine through other plants, hedges and fences, always growing in a clockwise direction. It is said that if the stems are untwined and forced to grow counter-clockwise, then the plant will perish, but it always manages to resume its natural direction. The flower bud is enclosed by two large, delicately veined bracts, which give rise to its scientific name *Calystegia*, which means 'beautiful covering'.

Field Bindweed is more of a pest to the farmer than the gardener, frequently sprawling along the ground and twining through crops. It is seen in arable fields, and on rough wasteground. The flower trumpets are smaller than Hedge Bindweed, often vividly coloured, pink with candy-stripes of white. Unlike Hedge Bindweed, the flowers are sensitive to light, only opening fully in sunshine, otherwise they remain rolled up.

Rough wasteland

Hedge Bindweed is a prolific and tenacious climber, which twines through hedges, along wire fences and even reaching up telegraph poles. It is easily recognized by the large white trumpet-shaped flowers which often decorate urban landscapes.

Field Bindweed sprawls or climbs over the ground or spirals more tightly around the stems of other vegetation like a coiled spring. The flowers are neatly rolled up in dull weather, but the pink and white variety is unmistakeable when fully open.

Hedge Bindweed

RANGE: Throughout Europe, except the far North

FLOWERING TIME
July to September

Field Bindweed

RANGE: Throughout Europe, except the far North

FLOWERING TIME
June to September

23

Chickweed / Common Mouse-ear

Chickweed
Stellaria media

The white flowers, each just 6-10 mm across, have five petals, but each so deeply-cleft in two, there appear to be ten. The five green sepals beneath are longer than the petals, and can be clearly seen between them.

Small, oval, hairless leaves are arranged in opposite pairs on a trailing stem, which has a single line of hairs along its length, the line changing position between each pair of leaves.

Common Mouse-ear
Cerastium fontanum

The small, oval and rather pointed leaves are covered in fine hairs and have a rather furry appearance. They are attached without stalks directly to the stem, which is itself clothed in fine hairs.

The flowers are white, sometimes with faint greyish lines, 6-10 mm across, and each petal is divided for about half way along its length. The sepals can be seen between each petal, but are just a little shorter.

Farmland

Chickweed is a very common plant of fields or disturbed ground, cultivated and wasteground or shingle beaches. Its cheerful tiny, starry flowers peer up to the sky at almost any time of year – the long flowering period is typical of many successful plants. At night, the leaves fold in towards the stem to protect the young buds. It has long been used as a tasty, though very small, salad vegetable, but was more frequently given to caged birds or chickens as a tonic; chickweed poultices were used to reduce swellings. Folklore has it that an infusion of chickweed is a remedy for obesity – unfortunately not founded in fact.

Common Mouse-ear is, at first glance, a very similar plant to Chickweed, and is almost as common in grassy places such as pastures and uncut lawns. But the very hairy leaves, like little mouse ears, immediately distinguish it. The green sepals below each flower are about the same size as the petals, unlike Chickweed's. As the tiny fruit capsule ripens and lengthens, it becomes curved, and the drying sepals curl back, so that the whole resembles a miniature half-peeled banana. Field Mouse-ear (*Cerastium arvense*) has much larger flowers.

Grassy meadows

24

Chickweed forms cushions of green between the crops in arable land, or creeps through long grass, producing pin-pricks of tiny white star-like flowers above bright green paired leaves.

Common Mouse-ear trails through grassland in exactly the same way, but the leaves are distinctly 'furry', and the whole plant has a looser, more untidy appearance.

Chickweed

RANGE: Throughout Europe

FLOWERING TIME
All year but mostly from March to November

Common Mouse-ear

RANGE: Throughout Europe

FLOWERING TIME
April to October

25

Wood Sorrel / Wood Anemone

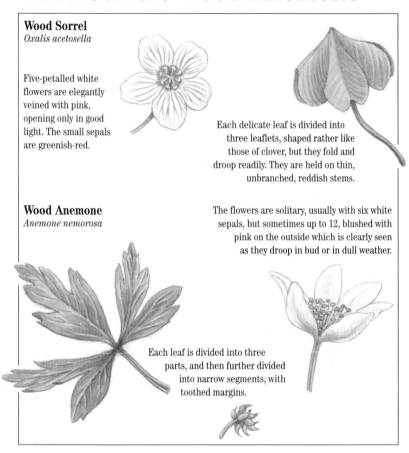

Wood Sorrel
Oxalis acetosella

Five-petalled white flowers are elegantly veined with pink, opening only in good light. The small sepals are greenish-red.

Each delicate leaf is divided into three leaflets, shaped rather like those of clover, but they fold and droop readily. They are held on thin, unbranched, reddish stems.

Wood Anemone
Anemone nemorosa

The flowers are solitary, usually with six white sepals, but sometimes up to 12, blushed with pink on the outside which is clearly seen as they droop in bud or in dull weather.

Each leaf is divided into three parts, and then further divided into narrow segments; with toothed margins.

Both species: woodland

The delicate and curiously shaped leaves of **Wood Sorrel** are very sensitive, drooping in strong sunshine to conserve moisture, or folding along the length of each leaflet like a closed umbrella at night. They have a sharp but refreshing acid taste, and have been used to enliven salads, and as a source of oxalic acid. Both parts of the scientific name reflect this: the Greek *Oxys* meaning acid, and *acetosella* meaning vinegar salts. The plant is also a strong diuretic and may not suit all constitutions. The flowers are as delicate as the leaves, and the plant tends to form dainty patches within deciduous or coniferous woodlands rather than great swathes. It also grows on mountains.

Wood Anemone, on the other hand, can create an enormous carpet across deciduous woodland or coppice floors in spring, the white flowers following the track of the sun across the sky, well before the leaf canopy of the trees shuts out the light. The 'petals' are in fact sepals, each blushed with pink on the outside. They droop gracefully before opening fully, and were said in mythology to spring from the tears of Venus, weeping over the death of Adonis. The plant is a member of the buttercup family, and the leaves resemble those of that plant. It also shares the poisonous nature of buttercups.

Wood Sorrel *is instantly recognizable by its little triad of bright yellow-green folded leaves, usually over the leaf-litter of a woodland floor. The cheerful pink-veined flowers are conspicuous but are not open for very long, though the leaves remain present well into the summer.*

Wood Anemone *is unmissable when in flower with its broad starry petals forming a white blanket over the ground – often punctuated with the yellow of primroses – and is almost as noticeable when the flowers are closed and blushing modestly with their pink undersides and delicate fern-like leaves.*

Wood Sorrel

RANGE: Throughout Europe

FLOWERING TIME
April to June

Wood Anemone

RANGE: Throughout Europe

FLOWERING TIME
March to May

27

Greater Stitchwort/Wild Strawberry

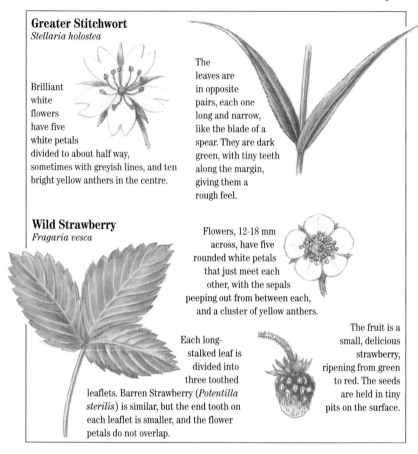

Greater Stitchwort
Stellaria holostea

Brilliant white flowers have five white petals divided to about half way, sometimes with greyish lines, and ten bright yellow anthers in the centre.

The leaves are in opposite pairs, each one long and narrow, like the blade of a spear. They are dark green, with tiny teeth along the margin, giving them a rough feel.

Wild Strawberry
Fragaria vesca

Flowers, 12-18 mm across, have five rounded white petals that just meet each other, with the sepals peeping out from between each, and a cluster of yellow anthers.

Each long-stalked leaf is divided into three toothed leaflets. Barren Strawberry (*Potentilla sterilis*) is similar, but the end tooth on each leaflet is smaller, and the flower petals do not overlap.

The fruit is a small, delicious strawberry, ripening from green to red. The seeds are held in tiny pits on the surface.

Both species: woodland

The bold white flowers of **Greater Stitchwort** brighten the way along woodland paths, clearings and shady hedge banks. It is a straggling plant with rather weak stems, relying on other spring-time vegetation for support, often growing among the tall grasses on the edge of a clearing. The plant remains in place long after flowering, and after the tree canopy has developed to enshroud the woodland in gloom, when the ranks of paired, narrow leaflets have a ladder-like appearance. Each leaf has minute teeth along its margin, which are difficult to see, but easily felt with a fingertip. Lesser Stitchwort (*Stellaria graminea*) has smaller leaves and flowers, and usually occurs in grassland.

Wild Strawberry occupies similar places in light woodland, paths and clearings, and may also be found on railway banks or rocky outcrops in upland areas, but it is easily passed by, as the small rose-like flowers often only just peep out from between the long-stalked leaves. The leaves have a long history of medicinal uses, particularly for digestive disorders. The fruits are tiny, but have a sweet delicate flavour, even finer than the cultivated variety which sometimes escapes into the wild. Strawberries are unusual in that the seeds are held on the outside of the fleshy part of the fruit.

Greater Stitchwort *is a bold plant, whose fairly large starry flowers show up in stark contrast to its regular rows of paired leaves – like stitches – in the dappled shade of its springtime habitat.*

Wild Strawberry *is a much more secretive plant, hugging the ground and sometimes hiding its attractive flowers among the three-lobed and strongly toothed, deeply-veined leaves, which are in many ways its most distinctive feature.*

Greater Stitchwort

RANGE: Throughout Europe, except the extreme North

FLOWERING TIME
April to June

Wild Strawberry

RANGE: Throughout Europe

FLOWERING TIME
April to July, in fruit from May to August

29

Pond Water-crowfoot / White Water-lily

Pond Water-crowfoot
Ranunculus peltatus

Flowers usually have five, occasionally up to seven, white petals with a yellow blotch and yellow anthers at the centre. They are 15-20 mm across.

The surface leaves are flat and divided into three to seven shallow lobes with rounded margins. Submerged leaves, or those of plants growing on muddy margins, are finely divided into numerous fine threads, like those of fennel.

White Water-lily
Nymphaea alba

Large white flowers, 100-200 mm across, with 20 or more petals and numerous yellow stamens, some of which have a flat white blade instead of the usual stalk or filament. These are called petaloid stamens.

The leaves are large and more or less rounded, divided almost to the middle where the stalk joins the leaf. Glossy green above, reddish-purple below.

*Both species:
ponds, ditches*

Pond Water-crowfoot is a white aquatic buttercup of freshwater ponds and ditches, with still or slow-moving water. There are many species in Europe, often exhibiting two different kinds of leaf. One remains submerged and is finely divided into threads; the other is flat and sits on the water surface. This species has both kinds of leaf, but if the pond dries up and becomes muddy, then only the thread-like leaves are produced. The plant can be abundant if conditions are right, and on a sunny day a pond may be covered with its large patches of pretty white flowers.

White water-lily is altogether much bigger and there is no danger of confusion between the two. The leaves may be the size of small dinner plates, and the many-petalled flowers, which sit directly on the water surface, are perhaps the largest of any European wild flower. They only open fully in sunshine: otherwise they are enclosed by the greenish-red sepals. When the flowers have been pollinated by small beetles, they sink below the surface again, where a large spongy fruit capsule develops unseen. The plant may grow so prolifically that the leaves are squeezed together, folding up to reveal their red undersides. It grows on freshwater ponds, lakes and large ditches with still water.

Pond Water-crow-foot's yellow centre to the flowers is only obvious when viewed close-up, and the shape of the floating leaves help to identify the species. A water surface covered in small white flowers is likely to have been colonized by Pond Water-crowfoot, or one of its many relatives.

White Water-lily is quite unmistakeable with its large, many-petalled flowers on the water surface. When not in flower, the rounded, rather than oblong, leaves distinguish it from Yellow Water-lily.

Pond Water-crowfoot

RANGE: Throughout Europe, except the extreme North

FLOWERING TIME
May to July

White Water-lily

RANGE: Throughout Europe, except the extreme North

FLOWERING TIME
June to September

Meadow Saxifrage / Grass of Parnassus

Meadow Saxifrage
Saxifraga granulata

The flowers, 20-30 mm across, have five white oval petals, often marked with greyish veins, and occur in branched clusters of up to 12.

The leaves, which are somewhat hairy, are kidney-shaped with a distinctive toothed edge, like cogs on a gear-wheel.

Leaves occur either on long stalks from the base, or clasp the flower stems tightly about one third of the way up their length. They are somewhat glossy, distinctly heart-shaped and strongly veined.

Grass of Parnassus
Parnassia palustris

Flowers are solitary – each with its own stem. They are 20-30 mm across, each petal with fine translucent veins. The centre of the flower has a round pinkish ovary, five yellow stamens and five yellow branched staminodes.

Meadow Saxifrage is taller and more robust than many of the other European saxifrages, which tend to occur in mountainous regions. The word 'saxifrage' means stone-breaker, referring to their habit of growing in the cracks and crevices of rocks. This species however, occurs among pastures, grassy road verges and grasses of lush meadows, producing a mass of pretty white flowers on branched stems. Apart from seed, it is also able to reproduce from tiny brown bulbils, clustered around the base of the stem.

Grassy meadows

Grass of Parnassus is a similar plant to Meadow Saxifrage. Its name comes from the Greek mountain where it was first found almost 2,000 years ago. The flower-stems are not branched like those of Meadow Saxifrages, and the leaves are distinctly heart-shaped. But its most distinguishing feature is the ring of five yellow 'staminodes' set against each petal. These are modified stamens, branched like the strings of a harp, and serve to attract pollinating insects to the flower and the true stamens, for they are infertile themselves. The base of each staminode secretes nectar, which can sometimes be seen glistening like a drop of honey. It can be found in wet pastures, fens and lush marshy-places.

Marshland

Meadow Saxifrage
*produces a mass of
many bright white
flowers on branched
stems at just above
ankle-height in old
meadows and
roadsides. The
distinctive leaves,
though, are the key
to identification.*

Grass of Parnassus
*has a similar general
appearance in many
ways, but is somewhat
fleshy and rather 'neat
and tidy', with its
solitary cupped
flowers on long stems.*

Meadow Saxifrage

Grass of Parnassus

RANGE: Almost throughout Europe, except the far North

RANGE: Almost throughout Europe

FLOWERING TIME
April to June

FLOWERING TIME
June to September

Cowberry/Broad-leaved Willowherb

Cowberry
Vaccinium vitis-idaea

Each flower is just 6-8 mm long, but there are always several clustered together. The tips of each of the four pinkish-white petals are curved slightly.

The fruit is an acid tasting, egg-shaped berry, which ripens from green to yellow to brilliant scarlet.

The oval leaves, which become wider towards the end, have a leathery appearance, glossy above and much paler below where it is dotted with tiny black glands. They have a small notch at the very tip, and the leaf margins are rolled under slightly.

Broad-leaved Willowherb
Epilobium montanum

Bright green leaves are oval and pointed with a toothed margin, and are arranged in opposite pairs on the square, reddish stems.

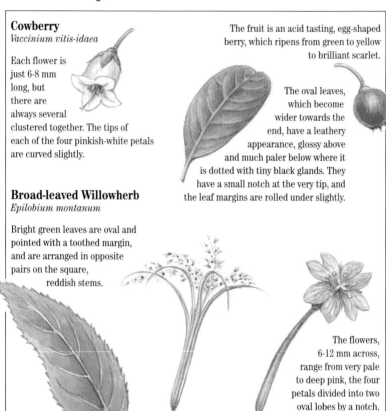

The flowers, 6-12 mm across, range from very pale to deep pink, the four petals divided into two oval lobes by a notch.

Heathland

Cowberry is a member of the heather family, closely related to the Bilberry (page 142), but with this species the flowers are of the palest pink. The four petals are fused together into a short tube, except that the tips of each are folded back slightly so that the flowers are like a cluster of little bells. Any similarity with Bilberry ends with the fruit: those of Cowberry are bright red, with a sharp, acid taste. It forms clumps of low bushes, usually not more than 50 cm high in upland areas such as moors, heaths and coniferous woods with acid soils.

Broad-leaved Willowherb is one of the commonest of the smaller willowherbs, whose leaves are just a little broader than the many other varieties, from which it is very difficult to tell apart. It is always a slender and seemingly fragile plant, and often looks rather sickly as the flower-buds droop in the shady corners of cultivated ground and waste-land, in which it prefers to grow. The flowers become upright as they open, and go on to develop long thin fruit capsules, splitting open along their length to reveal fluffy seeds, which are dispersed by the wind to enable the plant to establish itself almost anywhere.

Rough wasteland

Cowberry forms rounded, compact knee-high bushes which are dotted with clusters of the palest pink bells, and then later with red berries.

Broad-leaved Willowherb is an insignificant but common plant, slender and fragile, and noticeable for its very pale flowers which show up in the shady spots which it prefers.

Cowberry

Broad-leaved Willowherb

RANGE: Almost throughout Europe in upland areas

FLOWERING TIME
June to August

RANGE: Throughout Europe, except the far North

FLOWERING TIME
June to August

Field Rose/Dog Rose

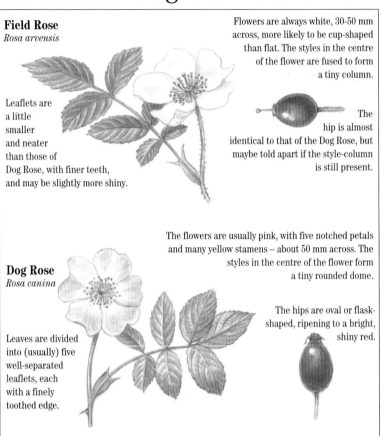

Field Rose
Rosa arvensis

Flowers are always white, 30-50 mm across, more likely to be cup-shaped than flat. The styles in the centre of the flower are fused to form a tiny column.

Leaflets are a little smaller and neater than those of Dog Rose, with finer teeth, and may be slightly more shiny.

The hip is almost identical to that of the Dog Rose, but maybe told apart if the style-column is still present.

Dog Rose
Rosa canina

The flowers are usually pink, with five notched petals and many yellow stamens – about 50 mm across. The styles in the centre of the flower form a tiny rounded dome.

The hips are oval or flask-shaped, ripening to a bright, shiny red.

Leaves are divided into (usually) five well-separated leaflets, each with a finely toothed edge.

Both species: hedgerows, roadsides

Nothing is more suggestive of the summer than a roadside hedge covered with roses. The **Field Rose** tends to form long trailing stems over hedgerow bushes and scrub, and produces a mass of white flowers, three or four on a stem, but usually with only one open at any time. The two species illustrated here are rather similar, but Field Rose can be distinguished by its smaller and neater leaves, and by the yellow styles in the centre of the flower, which are fused into a tiny little column. Both species sport vicious thorns on the stems.

Dog Rose flowers a little earlier than Field Rose, and usually, though not always, has pink flowers. The familiar rose hip is actually a swelling of that part of the stem which holds the flower: the true fruits are the hairy objects within, each containing one seed. Syrup made from the hips contains large amounts of vitamin C and has been made for centuries, but a tea can also be made from the leaves, indeed the plant is a cousin of the tea plant (*Camellia sinensis*) from which tea is usually made. Dog Rose may form free-standing bushes as well as trailing over other hedgerow plants, scrub and woodland margins.

Field Rose has a rather scrambling habit with long arching stems. The yellow anthers have usually turned brown by midday, but the column of styles in the centre is the key to identification.

Dog Rose is a more bushy plant, sometimes producing a greater abundance of flowers, and usually of the most delightful shade of pink. The flowering period is short, however, and is over far too soon.

Field Rose

Dog Rose

RANGE: Throughout southern and western Europe

FLOWERING TIME
June to August

RANGE: Throughout Europe, except the far North

FLOWERING TIME
June to July

Blackberry

Blackberry
Rubus fruticosus

The flowers have five petals which range from white to deep pink, usually well separated, with the green sepals visible between. They are 20-30 mm across and have numerous anthers, which quickly turn a dark colour and give the flowers a dirty appearance.

Each leaf is divided into three separate rather broad leaflets, sometimes with fine prickles on the veins underneath.

The familiar berry is actually a collection of fruits called drupelets, which ripen from green to red and finally to a shiny black. Dewberry (*Rubus caesius*) is a similar plant, but there are far fewer drupelets or segments to the berry, and they are covered in a bluish bloom.

Hedgerows, roadsides

Blackberry, or Bramble, is surely one of the most successful of plants. It can cope with a huge variety of habitats on a wide range of soils, and seems to be equally at home on the harsh, dry sands of a dune system as it is on the rich humus of sheltered woodland. It may exist in many different forms, too, in order to cope with different conditions: as a low prostrate plant hugging the ground, for example, or with long arching stems reaching high up over hedgerows and trees. It can be found in almost any habitat, but particularly wasteground, hedgerows and woods, avoiding very wet soils. The major reason for this success is that Blackberry is able to produce fertile seed without pollination with another plant, so a new plant is in effect a clone of its parent. Over millennia, mutations have occurred which are well adapted to various conditions, but the genetic make-up of these mutations remains very stable. Botanists call these mutations microspecies, and they explain why Blackberry flowers come in such a variety of colours, or why the fruit of some plants is sweet and delicious, while that of others is small and sour. The sharp thorns that line the stems of Blackberry also contribute to its success, for they prevent the plant from being easily grazed.

Blackberry is an extremely variable plant, but is hard to miss as the thorns so readily attach themselves to clothing, or even bare skin. The flowers, often in profusion, always appear grubbier and less tidy than those of the roses which have larger, neater flowers. The edible fruits, which may appear at the same time as the flowers, are unmistakeable.

Blackberry

RANGE: Throughout Europe,
except the far North

FLOWERING TIME
May to November

39

Field Pansy/Scentless Mayweed

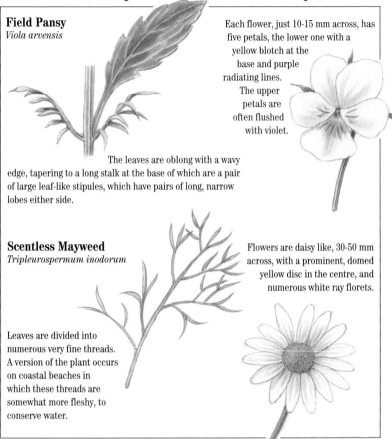

Field Pansy
Viola arvensis

Each flower, just 10-15 mm across, has five petals, the lower one with a yellow blotch at the base and purple radiating lines. The upper petals are often flushed with violet.

The leaves are oblong with a wavy edge, tapering to a long stalk at the base of which are a pair of large leaf-like stipules, which have pairs of long, narrow lobes either side.

Scentless Mayweed
Tripleurospermum inodorum

Flowers are daisy like, 30-50 mm across, with a prominent, domed yellow disc in the centre, and numerous white ray florets.

Leaves are divided into numerous very fine threads. A version of the plant occurs on coastal beaches in which these threads are somewhat more fleshy, to conserve water.

Both species: farmland

Both these plants are common weeds of arable fields, abandoned farmland, wasteground and disturbed bare ground, but are very different in character. **Field Pansy** is a small and slender plant, often hidden between stalks of corn but usually on patches of bare soil. The flowers are small and sometimes hidden, folded up within the sepals that surround them, but open fully when the sun shines. Although the flowers may have purple tinges on the upper petals, plants with much larger purple and yellow flowers are those of Wild Pansy (*Viola tricolor*), which grows in similar situations.

Scentless Mayweed is a robust weed with large daisy-like flowers, and leaves divided into fine threads. There are several similar species such as Scented Mayweed (*Matricaria recutita*), which has a pleasant chamomile fragrance when the leaves are crushed. Once the two have been distinguished, it becomes easier to spot the difference visually, as Scentless Mayweed is a bushier, lusher plant with larger flowers whose white rays do not droop so readily. It is related to Chamomile (*Chamaemelum nobile*) which is much smaller and prefers sandy, grazed heaths, and although Scented Mayweed has been used medicinally, it does not share Chamomile's famous healing properties.

Field Pansy usually hides between the crops or weeds of arable land, and is a small leafy plant with flowers that open shyly from within the large sepals that surround them.

Scentless Mayweed forms compact, domed clumps – easily seen from any distance – and is more leafy and floriferous than many of the similar daisy-like plants that frequent wasteground.

Field Pansy

RANGE: Throughout Europe, except the far North

FLOWERING TIME
May to October

Scentless Mayweed

RANGE: Throughout Europe

FLOWERING TIME
July to September

41

Daisy/Oxeye Daisy

Daisy
Bellis perennis

The flowers
are 15-20 mm
across. The underside
of the white rays are
usually flushed deep
pink, very noticeable when
in bud, and are surrounded
at the base by a ring of hairy
green bracts.

The leaves
are shaped like
a spoon, covered with
fine hairs, and lie flat to the
ground in a tight rosette.

The flowers are 30-50 mm across, not pink
under the white rays, but with a supporting
structure of green bracts, which protect the
flowers from insects biting their way through
the petals to get to the nectar at the base.

Oxeye Daisy
Leucanthemum vulgare

Lower
leaves are
spoon-shaped
with deep lobes, but
upper leaves are more
deeply-divided with
long teeth, and clasp the
flower stem at their base.

*Both species:
grassy meadows*

The **Daisy** is familiar to everyone, not least because it so readily appears in lawns and close-cut or grazed grassland everywhere. It avoids very wet places. The leaves grow in a tight rosette close to the ground and so avoid the blades of the mower, and their acrid taste makes the plant unpalatable to grazing animals and most insects. Moreover, its ability to flower for such an extended period from early spring to late autumn means that it reproduces freely. There was a superstition that Daisies boiled in milk and given to puppies would prevent them from growing any bigger.

Oxeye Daisy is similar, except that it is very much bigger, though sometimes in harsh conditions or where the vegetation has been cut it may be quite short. However the flower-heads remain large. The flower-head, like the Daisy's, is composed of many tiny yellow disc-florets, each a complete flower in itself. These are surrounded by ray florets, with each ray also being a complete flower. The plant favours meadows, lightly grazed pastures, road verges and embankments, and is quick to colonize open ground. In recent years, the similar Shasta Daisy (*Leucanthemum x superbum*), with much larger flowers, has been on the increase, as its seeds have been sown on motorway embankments.

Daisy *is the unmistakeable flower of lawns and short pastures, never more than ankle-high. It can sometimes be so abundant as to colour entire fields white.*

Oxeye Daisy, *usually knee-high or even taller, and with its large top-heavy flowers swaying in the breeze, may create an impressive display, especially along road verges.*

Daisy

RANGE: Throughout Europe, except the far North

FLOWERING TIME
May to October

Oxeye Daisy

RANGE: Throughout Europe

FLOWERING TIME
June to August

43

Black Nightshade / Eyebright

Black Nightshade
Solanum nigrum

Eyebright
Euphrasia officinalis agg.

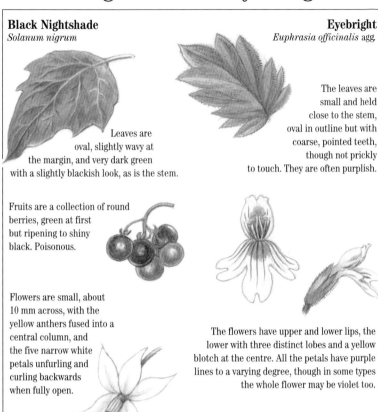

The leaves are small and held close to the stem, oval in outline but with coarse, pointed teeth, though not prickly to touch. They are often purplish.

Leaves are oval, slightly wavy at the margin, and very dark green with a slightly blackish look, as is the stem.

Fruits are a collection of round berries, green at first but ripening to shiny black. Poisonous.

Flowers are small, about 10 mm across, with the yellow anthers fused into a central column, and the five narrow white petals unfurling and curling backwards when fully open.

The flowers have upper and lower lips, the lower with three distinct lobes and a yellow blotch at the centre. All the petals have purple lines to a varying degree, though in some types the whole flower may be violet too.

Farmland

Black Nightshade is a member of the potato family, and is frequently found among crops of potatoes, though it occurs on cultivated fields and wasteground generally. It is an annual and can take advantage quickly of any recently disturbed ground, and so has spread throughout much of the globe. The flowers are very similar to those of potato, though much smaller, with their central column of yellow anthers fused together, and narrow white petals recurving backwards. The whole plant, and especially the berries, are poisonous.

For centuries **Eyebright** has been held in great esteem for curing disorders of the eyes, and its effectiveness as a treatment was thought to be signified by the yellow spots and purple lines in the white of the flower, resembling diseased eyes. It is a semi-parasitic plant deriving some of its nutrient from the roots of grasses among which it grows. It may be very short or taller and more bushy, and the flower colour ranges from white to dark purple. It favours pastures and other grasslands, heaths and woodland clearings. Many species and hybrids have been identified, but they are difficult to separate, so *Euphrasia officinalis* aggregate is a useful term encompassing most of the European species.

Grassy meadows

Black Nightshade *is a rather grubby-looking plant of farmland, looking like an impoverished potato but with small, pretty white flowers dotted about its form, and leaves that sometimes appear over-sized.*

Eyebright *can be inconspicuous when it is short, with only the flowers peeping out of the surrounding grass, but when it is taller the purple-tinged leaves draw the eye to the beautifully delicate flowers.*

Black Nightshade

RANGE: Throughout Europe, except the far North

FLOWERING TIME
June to October

Eyebright

RANGE: Throughout Europe

FLOWERING TIME
July to September

45

White Dead-nettle / Wood Sage

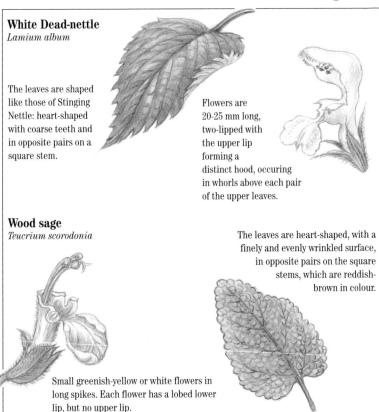

White Dead-nettle
Lamium album

The leaves are shaped like those of Stinging Nettle: heart-shaped with coarse teeth and in opposite pairs on a square stem.

Flowers are 20-25 mm long, two-lipped with the upper lip forming a distinct hood, occuring in whorls above each pair of the upper leaves.

Wood sage
Teucrium scorodonia

The leaves are heart-shaped, with a finely and evenly wrinkled surface, in opposite pairs on the square stems, which are reddish-brown in colour.

Small greenish-yellow or white flowers in long spikes. Each flower has a lobed lower lip, but no upper lip.

White Dead-nettle is a common plant of road verges, hedgerows and woodland margins, that is easy to recognize as soon as it bursts into flower. But until that happens, the harmless leaves alone look remarkably like those of the Stinging Nettle, with which *Hedgerows, roadsides* it often grows, although the two are quite unrelated. No doubt this resemblance helps to protect the plant from being grazed or even pulled up as a weed. The whorls of large white, two-lipped flowers are visited by bumble bees, which have the body weight to push apart the lips of the flower and reach the nectar at their base.

Wood Sage, like White Dead-nettle, is a member of the mint family, but it is not a true sage. The flowers are creamy-white or yellow-green, with a lobed lower lip but no upper lip, so that the brown stamens are exposed. The real key to the identification of this plant however are the wrinkled, heart-shaped leaves, and its habitat of dry sandy soils on heaths, grasslands and open woods. It has a bitter taste and smells similar to hops, and has been used for flavouring beer, as well as a remedy for bruises and various other ailments.

Heathland

White Dead-nettle *generally has a rather neat, tidy and lush appearance, usually about 30 cm high and in small clumps. The large flowers separate it from any other white-flowered member of the mint family.*

Wood Sage *is a slightly taller but much less leafy plant, especially in the upper part, with several thin wiry stems reaching up. These are almost knobbly in appearance, with tightly arranged, small creamy flowers.*

White Dead-nettle

RANGE: Throughout Europe, except the far North

FLOWERING TIME
April to November

Wood Sage

RANGE: Throughout western Europe, except the far North

FLOWERING TIME
June to September

Honeysuckle / Traveller's-joy

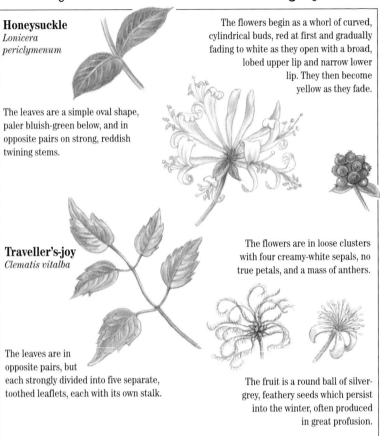

Honeysuckle
Lonicera
periclymenum

The flowers begin as a whorl of curved, cylindrical buds, red at first and gradually fading to white as they open with a broad, lobed upper lip and narrow lower lip. They then become yellow as they fade.

The leaves are a simple oval shape, paler bluish-green below, and in opposite pairs on strong, reddish twining stems.

Traveller's-joy
Clematis vitalba

The flowers are in loose clusters with four creamy-white sepals, no true petals, and a mass of anthers.

The leaves are in opposite pairs, but each strongly divided into five separate, toothed leaflets, each with its own stalk.

The fruit is a round ball of silver-grey, feathery seeds which persist into the winter, often produced in great profusion.

Both species: hedgerows, roadsides

The sweet scent of **Honeysuckle** is most noticeable on still summer evenings, when it attracts moths to pollinate its flowers; during the day they are visited by bees for their abundant nectar. They are arranged in whorls or clusters of up to 12, and go through a change of colours as they ripen from red to peach to white and finally creamy-yellowish. The clusters of berries also change, from green to red. This is a plant of hedgerows and woodland that depends on other vegetation for support, sometimes creeping along the ground, sometimes climbing high into a tree before bushing out.

Traveller's-joy is another plant that clambers over hedgerows and through woodlands. It may form thick woody stems which hang down from the trees like jungle lianas, with the bark peeling off in strips, and can be recognized well into the winter by the persistent globes of fluffy, silvery-grey seeds which are draped over the bare branches of the hedgerow. Rather surprisingly, it is a member of the buttercup family, and in common with other members it possesses an acrid, irritating juice. In central and eastern Europe the similar Erect Clematis (*Clematis recta*) occurs as a low bushy plant that does not climb over other vegetation.

Honeysuckle *is a climbing and trailing plant with large whorls or 'candelabras' of sweet-scented flowers in a range of creamy-yellow colours.*

*****Traveller's-joy*** *is also a climbing plant but with masses of small white flowers in summer and clouds of silver feathery seeds in winter.*

Honeysuckle

RANGE: Western Europe

FLOWERING TIME
June to September

Traveller's-joy

RANGE: Western Europe,
avoiding the North

FLOWERING TIME
July to September

White Clover / Hairy Bittercress

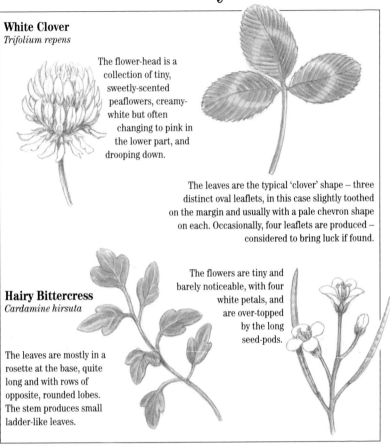

White Clover
Trifolium repens

The flower-head is a collection of tiny, sweetly-scented peaflowers, creamy-white but often changing to pink in the lower part, and drooping down.

The leaves are the typical 'clover' shape – three distinct oval leaflets, in this case slightly toothed on the margin and usually with a pale chevron shape on each. Occasionally, four leaflets are produced – considered to bring luck if found.

Hairy Bittercress
Cardamine hirsuta

The flowers are tiny and barely noticeable, with four white petals, and are over-topped by the long seed-pods.

The leaves are mostly in a rosette at the base, quite long and with rows of opposite, rounded lobes. The stem produces small ladder-like leaves.

Grassy meadows

White Clover is commonly seen on lawns and short grassland everywhere, but is also sometimes sown on pastures to improve the soil (it adds nitrogen through the action of bacteria in the roots); it is also a fodder crop for cattle. Each of the tiny white flowers in the flower-head hold a drop of nectar at the base, which may be tasted if they are pulled off one by one. The lowermost flowers in the head often droop down as the flowers age, taking on a pinkish tinge, to form a little petticoat below the others. The plant spreads rapidly by long, creeping stems that form new roots at intervals.

Hairy Bittercress is one of those plants that is easily overlooked, but can be found almost anywhere on farmland, waste-places and gardens, wherever the soil has been disturbed or there is little competition, including pavement cracks and on old walls. The tiny white flowers are soon outgrown by the lengthening fruit capsules, which, when ripe, burst open at the slightest touch, audibly scattering the seeds some distance. The fresh young leaves, though small, make a tangy addition to salads.

Rough wasteland

White clover creeps over the ground, rarely more than ankle-high, and produces masses of rounded flower-heads, starting out white and gradually taking on a pinkish tinge.

Hairy Bittercress is an insignificant weed of urban areas. It is short and slender, with the tiniest flowers and long, thin seed-pods reaching upward.

White Clover

RANGE: Throughout Europe

FLOWERING TIME
June to September

Hairy Bittercress

RANGE: Throughout Europe,
except the North

FLOWERING TIME
March to October

51

Shepherd's-purse/Field Penny-cress

Shepherd's-purse
Capsella bursa-pastoris

The flowers are tiny, just 2 mm across, with four white petals. They form in a cluster at the top of long stems.

The leaves are mostly in a rosette at the base of the plant, deeply lobed and quite hairy.

The fruits appear alternately up the stems, each heart-shaped or triangular with a notch at the tip, and flattened on either side.

Field Penny-cress
Thlaspi arvense

The leaves are oblong and coarsely toothed, with a slightly waxy feel, and clasp the stem at their base.

The flowers are very similar to those of Shepherd's-purse, though slightly larger and showier.

The fruits are rounded, with broad, disc-like wings, and a small notch at the tip. Up to 15 mm across.

Shepherd's-purse is a ubiquitous, annual weed found almost everywhere in wasteland, fields, road verges and gardens. The seeds can germinate at any time of year in some locations, and the plant can be found in flower almost continuously, except in the harshest winter weather. When the curiously heart-shaped seed-pods begin to ripen and turn reddish-brown, they resemble the leather pouches carried by medieval shepherds, which is reflected in the Latin name *bursa-pastoris*. It is a variable plant, very short when growing in poor soils, but may be tall and lush when growing among crops on farmland.

Rough wasteland

Field Penny-cress tends to be restricted to the rich cultivated soils of farms. At first sight, it appears rather similar to Shepherd's-purse, but as the fruits develop they form wide membranous wings either side of the round seed-pod, with a small notch at the top. These are semi-translucent, and when the sun shines through them in the late evening they appear like yellow coins. Some species of penny-cress accumulate poisonous metals such as zinc and lead within their tissues, and may prove to be useful in cleansing toxic waste sites.

Farmland

Shepherd's-purse *is a familiar weed of disturbed soils that can be anything from ankle- to knee-height, easily recognized by the long spikes of tiny heart-shaped fruits.*

Field Penny-cress *is a similar but more robust, leafier and fleshier plant, with more tightly-packed columns of disc-shaped fruits.*

Shepherd's-purse

RANGE: Throughout Europe

FLOWERING TIME
All year, depending
on weather conditions

Field Penny-cress

RANGE: Throughout Europe

FLOWERING TIME
May to August

Ramsons/Garlic Mustard

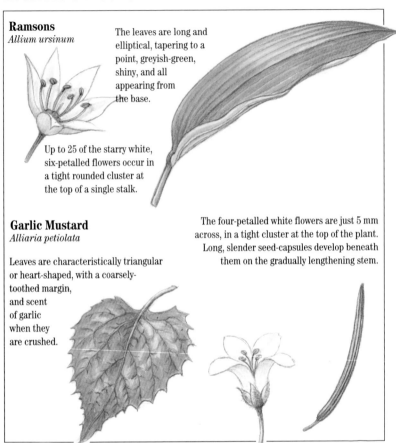

Ramsons
Allium ursinum

The leaves are long and elliptical, tapering to a point, greyish-green, shiny, and all appearing from the base.

Up to 25 of the starry white, six-petalled flowers occur in a tight rounded cluster at the top of a single stalk.

Garlic Mustard
Alliaria petiolata

The four-petalled white flowers are just 5 mm across, in a tight cluster at the top of the plant. Long, slender seed-capsules develop beneath them on the gradually lengthening stem.

Leaves are characteristically triangular or heart-shaped, with a coarsely-toothed margin, and scent of garlic when they are crushed.

Woodland

Both of these plants are characterized by their smell of garlic, though they are unrelated. **Ramsons** is a member of the onion family, and may form great carpets over a large area in damp woodland or shady banks in spring, often to the exclusion of other plants, though in the mild climates of the far west it appears out in the open among rocks. The scent of the leaves and flowers can be almost overpowering on warm, still days, but the taste of the leaves is milder than their fragrance suggests, and they make an excellent addition to salads.

Garlic Mustard is a member of the cress family, flowering at the same time as Ramsons but preferring roadsides, hedge banks and woodland edges where there is dappled shade. Its scent is not nearly so powerful, and the leaves must be crushed to release the aroma. It is a very attractive plant when young, but as the small cluster of flowers at the top begins to set fruit, the stems lengthen as the ripening pods develop, and the plant becomes lanky as though it has outgrown itself. If used for culinary purposes, the leaves should be collected when they are still young.

Hedgerows, roadsides

Ramsons forms swathes of greyish leaves in spring, followed by rounded 'pom-poms' of starry flowers like white lollipops, which fill the air with a heady garlic scent.

Garlic Mustard, though knee-high or taller, is a soft and fragile plant forming clumps in the dappled light of woodland margins, whose clusters of white flowers seem small compared to the coarsely-toothed leaves.

Ramsons

RANGE: Western Europe

FLOWERING TIME
Flowers for about three weeks
between late April to early June

Garlic Mustard

RANGE: Throughout Europe,
except the far North

FLOWERING TIME
Flowers from April to June

Water-cress/Cuckooflower

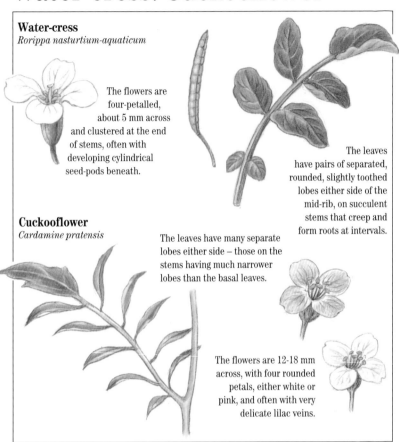

Water-cress
Rorippa nasturtium-aquaticum

The flowers are four-petalled, about 5 mm across and clustered at the end of stems, often with developing cylindrical seed-pods beneath.

The leaves have pairs of separated, rounded, slightly toothed lobes either side of the mid-rib, on succulent stems that creep and form roots at intervals.

Cuckooflower
Cardamine pratensis

The leaves have many separate lobes either side – those on the stems having much narrower lobes than the basal leaves.

The flowers are 12-18 mm across, with four rounded petals, either white or pink, and often with very delicate lilac veins.

Ponds, ditches

Water-cress is easily identified by its four cress-type petals when in flower. It is found at the margins of fast-flowing streams or in ditches and ponds. The green parts, however, are very similar to some other species, particularly of the carrot family, whose stems and leaves have the same succulent appearance. Water-cress and its various hybrids are the same as Water-cress sold commercially and used in salads, but it should not be collected in the wild for culinary use unless it is thoroughly cooked: it may contain the larvae of liver flukes which can infect humans as well as cattle and sheep.

Cuckooflower is a related plant which makes a delightful springtime sight in wet meadows and roadsides. The flowers range in colour from the very palest pink to mauve, and large areas may be coloured by them where extensive colonies are formed. The lower leaves at the base are rather similar in form to those of Water-cress, but further up the stem they are finer, with narrow lobes either side. In Great Britain, the date that the flowers are fully in bloom is associated with the first date that the call of the

Marshland

56

Water-cress *is a succulent plant that always has its feet in water, growing to somewhere between ankle- and knee-height. The four-petalled flowers distinguish it from other plants with similar leaves.*

Cuckooflower *may form small clumps or large colonies of delightful pink or white flowers, usually growing not much higher than the surrounding grass in damp meadows.*

Water-cress	Cuckooflower

RANGE: Throughout Europe, except for much of Scandinavia	**RANGE:** Throughout Europe
FLOWERING TIME May to October	**FLOWERING TIME** April to June

Bladder Campion/White Campion

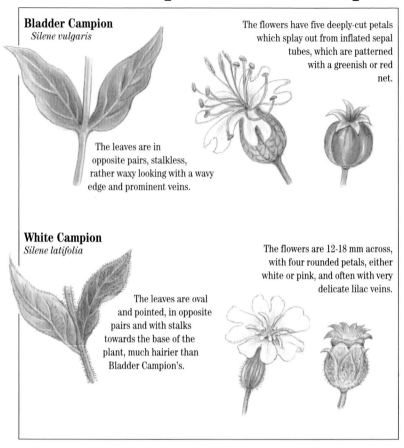

Bladder Campion
Silene vulgaris

The flowers have five deeply-cut petals which splay out from inflated sepal tubes, which are patterned with a greenish or red net.

The leaves are in opposite pairs, stalkless, rather waxy looking with a wavy edge and prominent veins.

White Campion
Silene latifolia

The flowers are 12-18 mm across, with four rounded petals, either white or pink, and often with very delicate lilac veins.

The leaves are oval and pointed, in opposite pairs and with stalks towards the base of the plant, much hairier than Bladder Campion's.

Both species: grassy meadows

These two closely related species seem to be very similar, but once seen they are easily distinguished. **Bladder Campion** is found on field margins, road verges and rough grassland in chalk or limestone areas. It is easily recognized by the inflated, balloon-like tube of sepals below the rather frilly petals, and the leaves are intricately patterned with a network of green or red veins. The 'bladders' sometimes have a small hole in the side where an insect has bitten through to reach the nectar, and the plant is often covered with 'cuckoo-spit' – the froth produced by froghopper bugs. In the evening, the flowers produce a fragrance like that of cloves, attracting pollinating moths.

White Campion occurs in similar situations, but has a rather more robust appearance, with petals which are not so deeply-cut, and straight-sided, rather hairy sepals. It is closely related to Red Campion, and where the two occur together a pink-flowered hybrid is produced. In strong sunshine, the petals curl up, and again a fragrance is produced only in the evening. Nottingham Catchfly (*Silene nutans*) is a related species with narrow petals that curl up completely during the day, so the plant looks almost dead, but they open wide as dusk falls in order to attract night-flying moths.

Bladder Campion *has an airy, lacy appearance created by the finely cut petals and the pale green, red or straw-coloured 'bladders' bobbing in the breeze, usually not more than kneehigh.*

White Campion *is often taller, with a more robust appearance generally, the large, pure white petals creating a stark contrast to the surrounding vegetation.*

Bladder Campion

RANGE: Throughout Europe

FLOWERING TIME
May to August

White Campion

RANGE: Throughout Europe, except northern Scandinavia and most of Ireland

FLOWERING TIME
May to September

Bogbean

Bogbean
Menyanthes trifoliata

The flowers have five hair-fringed petals, flushed pink on the outside, held in a tight cluster at the top of thick, leafless stems.

Leaves in groups of three, oval and pointed, somewhat leathery, usually held vertically.

The fruits are small round capsules, usually fewer in number than the flowers that preceded them (see above right).

Marshland

Bogbean is a curious plant with very specific habitat requirements: it only grows in shallow open pools where the water is rather acidic, such as found on peat bogs. On the moors and bogs of northern Europe it can be quite prolific, producing hundreds or even thousands of plants rising up out of the water from the long creeping stems which trail through the mud, and so forms colonies where conditions exist in which most plants find it difficult to grow. In spite of this, Bogbean often survives quite well in garden ponds where it provides attractive springtime interest. The leaves appear out of the water in groups of three, rather fleshy and bearing a strong resemblance to those of the garden or broad bean. They were once used as a cure for scurvy and for flavouring beer, and have also proved useful in treating skin diseases. The cluster of white flowers at the top of thick stems is extraordinary, for each petal is covered in thick white hairs which give them a feathery appearance, whilst the unopened buds have a delicate pink flush on the outside. They are followed by the fruit, which is a green egg-shaped capsule. A closely related plant of quite different appearance is the Fringed Water-lily (*Nymphoides peltata*), which has small round floating leaves and bright yellow five-petalled flowers, with each petal fringed with tiny hairs.

Bogbean only occurs in the acid pools of bogs and moors, often with no other plants visible. The sight of Bogbean en masse, *with its white blossoms dotted over the surface of the water, is unmistakeable. Little clusters of leaves in threes point directly upwards out of the water. These are followed by candelabras of delicate, feathery flowers.*

Bogbean

RANGE: Throughout Europe
in suitable habitats

FLOWERING TIME
May to July

Enchanter's nightshade Vervain

Enchanter's nightshade
Circaea lutetiana

Leaves are in opposite pairs, oval and with a finely-toothed margin and reddish veins.

The flowers have two tiny, heart-shaped petals, white or palest pink, and two prominent red-tipped stamens.

Vervain
Verbena officinalis

The leaves are deeply lobed and toothed, in opposite pairs on very tough stems.

The flowers are pale pink or lilac, with five petals which are slightly unequal on close examination, opening at the bottom of the spike first and working their way up to the top.

Woodland

Enchanter's nightshade is a plant of shady, secret places, in damp woods, at the foot of old walls or neglected corners of the garden. It is an uncharacteristic member of the willowherb family: instead of the usual fluffy seeds which are dispersed by the wind it produces small bristly capsules on drooping stalks which catch on animal fur and clothing. Though the two-petalled flowers are tiny, they show up remarkably well in the gloom of its favoured habitat, and this is one of the few woodland plants to flower in midsummer when the tree canopy has cast its deepest shade.

By contrast, **Vervain** prefers sunny situations and is typical of roadsides and rough places. The flowers are just as tiny, but are produced in slender spikes at the end of tough wiry stems which splay out like a candelabra.

It is recommended for a wide range of medicinal uses, and has been venerated as a magic charm for many centuries. A special incantation was recited whenever it was picked, and it would be carried when going on a long journey to protect against snake-bite and other misfortunes.

Rough wasteland

Enchanter's nightshade is an almost insignificant and fragile plant of shady places, but whose tiny white flowers show up brightly in the gloom.

Vervain is a robust and wiry plant, usually about knee-high with a mass of leaves in the lower part, and thin branched stems reaching up above, which are only sparsely covered with the tiny pink flowers.

Enchanter's nightshade

RANGE: Throughout Europe, avoiding Scandinavia

FLOWERING TIME
June to August

Vervain

RANGE: Throughout Europe, except the North

FLOWERING TIME
June to October

Japanese Knotweed/Indian Balsam

Japanese Knotweed
Fallopia japonica

Tiny, creamy-white flowers in pendent, branching spikes, produced from the base of the upper leaves (see below left).

Large heart-shaped leaves, appearing alternately on long, arching zig-zag stems almost 2 m tall (see right).

Indian Balsam
Impatiens glandulifera

The seed-pods burst open on the slightest touch when ripe, the segments rolling back suddenly to shower the seeds over many metres.

Elliptical leaves with a toothed margin and prominent reddish veins, in whorls of two to four, on succulent, juicy red-lined stems.

The flowers appear two-lipped, in a variety of shades from white to purple, with a curious opalescent, hooked sepal tube behind the petals.

Rough wasteland

Both these plants, introduced into Europe from Asia, can form large, invasive colonies on roadsides and wasteground, often obliterating the native vegetation. In the 19th century, gardeners held **Japanese Knotweed** in great esteem for its heart-shaped leaves and pretty spires of tiny white flowers, but now it is regarded as a serious pest: planting it deliberately is illegal in some countries. It spreads easily by long creeping roots, and the smallest fragment of root is able to sprout and form a new colony. It is also able to withstand repeated applications of chemical herbicides. Japanese Knotweed is edible: the young shoots and leaves are cooked in the same way as spinach; however the juice is a little sharp.

Indian Balsam is an annual, spreading rapidly by seed, and in spite of its invasive nature it is sometimes sown deliberately in the countryside for its eye-catching appearance. It is a tall, attractive plant that grows beside rivers and waterways, with large flowers produced in every shade of pink. As the long, spindle-shaped seed-pods become ripe, they dry out under tension, and split open explosively, propelling the seeds a considerable distance, often into the water where they float downstream to start a new colony.

Ponds, ditches

Japanese Knotweed *forms large, dense colonies on wasteground, much taller than head-high, giving the appearance of a bamboo, but with heart-shaped leaves.*

Indian Balsam *also forms dense colonies, though only next to water, and is just as tall, but has a succulent and fragile appearance, with brightly-coloured flowers that can be seen at any distance.*

Japanese Knotweed

RANGE: Throughout much of Europe and spreading rapidly

FLOWERING TIME
July to October

Indian Balsam

RANGE: Temperate Europe, avoiding the North and Mediterranean

FLOWERING TIME
July to September

Cleavers/Hedge Bedstraw

Cleavers
Galium aparine

Tiny flowers, 1.5 mm across, in small clusters among the young leaves.

The leaves are in whorls of six or more, rather long and narrow, and lined with backward pointing bristles, on long trailing stems.

Hedge Bedstraw
Galium mollugo

Leaves smaller and broader than Cleavers', almost hairless, on smooth stems which are square in cross section.

Huge, frothy clusters of flowers like candy floss. Each tiny flower has four pointed petals. The tiny round fruits turn black when ripe (see far left).

Rough wasteland

Cleavers or Goosegrass announces its presence by sticking itself on to clothes or animal fur with remarkable tenacity. Both the neat whorls of leaves and the long, trailing stems are lined with hooked hairs that grip fabric easily, though the plant itself may remain hidden among a tangle of nettles or tall grasses. It grows rapidly, up to 3 m in a season, but easily forms new colonies because the tiny, round double fruits are also covered in hooked bristles which latch effortlessly on to walkers. The plant is used as food for poultry, and may be eaten by humans – if cooked, the bristles become soft.

Hedge Bedstraw is a related plant that forms great frothy masses of creamy-white flowers on grasslands and road verges in summer, though each individual flower is only 2 mm across. The stems are quite unlike those of Cleavers: they are smooth. The leaves are much smaller, with a very finely toothed margin which can just be felt as a slight roughness. There are many species of Bedstraw in Europe, mostly smaller than this one, but they all yield a red dye from the roots.

Grassy meadows

Cleavers is a messy, higgledy-piggledy plant that grows in all directions at once, creating a tangle among other vegetation. The tiny flowers almost go unnoticed.

Hedge Bedstraw is a scrambling plant that forms a heap of creamy-white flowers like great frothy masses of foam on roadsides and hedge banks.

Cleavers	*Hedge Bedstraw*

RANGE: Throughout Europe except the far North	**RANGE:** Throughout Europe except much of Scandinavia
FLOWERING TIME May to September	**FLOWERING TIME** June to September

Meadowsweet

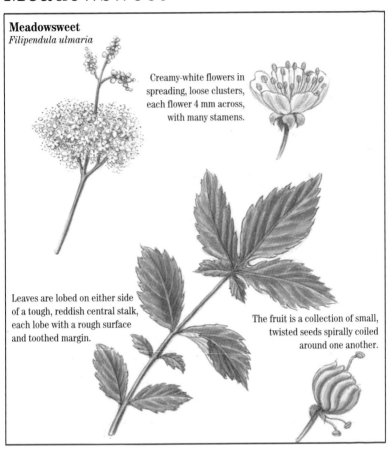

Meadowsweet
Filipendula ulmaria

Creamy-white flowers in spreading, loose clusters, each flower 4 mm across, with many stamens.

Leaves are lobed on either side of a tough, reddish central stalk, each lobe with a rough surface and toothed margin.

The fruit is a collection of small, twisted seeds spirally coiled around one another.

Marshland

Meadowsweet is a delightful herb of moist grassland and riversides that produces graceful, delicate tufts of creamy-white blooms throughout the summer months. The loose, frothy sprays of flowers may at first sight be taken for a member of the carrot family, but this plant is actually related to the rose.

The leaves produce a cucumber scent, but the flowers have the heady, almost sickly fragrance of honey and almonds, and were used for 'strewing' the floors of 16th century homes to impart a sweet scent and drive away insects. The little round drop-like buds contain salicylic acid and were first used for synthesizing aspirin, indeed a tea made from the flowers makes an excellent mild painkiller. The leaves have been shown to reduce the ulcers sometimes caused by pure aspirin. The flowers are still sometimes used for flavouring beer, and in particular it was used to season honey wine, or mead.

The scientific name *ulmaria* is a reference to the leaves' similarity to those of the Elm (*Ulmus*), not in terms of their general shape, but to the rough textured and wrinkled surface, which is very comparable to that of the Elm tree.

Meadowsweet often grows chest-high in the lush vegetation of marshy meadows or along a river bank, and is easily recognized by the irregularly shaped foamy clusters of flowers, like candy-floss on a stick. It often grows in great masses and stands tall above other vegetation.

Meadowsweet

RANGE: Throughout Europe

FLOWERING TIME
June to September

Yarrow/Sneezewort

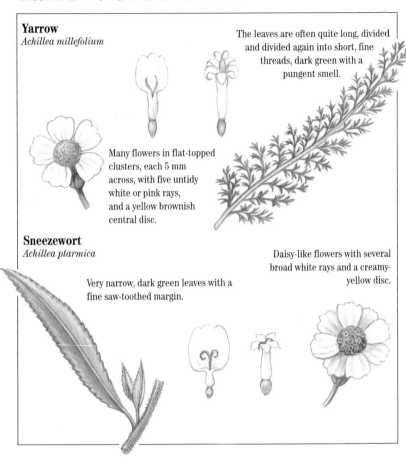

Yarrow
Achillea millefolium

The leaves are often quite long, divided and divided again into short, fine threads, dark green with a pungent smell.

Many flowers in flat-topped clusters, each 5 mm across, with five untidy white or pink rays, and a yellow brownish central disc.

Sneezewort
Achillea ptarmica

Very narrow, dark green leaves with a fine saw-toothed margin.

Daisy-like flowers with several broad white rays and a creamy-yellow disc.

Both species: grassy meadows

Yarrow is a common plant often found in lawns, meadows and other grassy places. It is very resilient and may be found in full bloom even when drought has coloured the lawn brown. The very finely divided leaves (the scientific name *millefoium* means a thousand leaves), which are immediately recognizable even when young, are extremely pungent, and are believed both to cause a nose bleed and to staunch an existing one. The flat-topped clusters of flowers may be white or pink, but as they mature, the anthers become brown and give the flowers a rather dirty appearance.

Sneezewort is the more attractive cousin of Yarrow, whose flowers are more daisy-like in appearance, with larger greenish-yellow central discs. It prefers damper habitats than Yarrow, such as wet meadows and marshes on slightly acid soils. The leaves are much narrower, without the fine multiple divisions of Yarrow, but with an attractive, delicately toothed margin. It is said that any part of the plant is likely to induce a sneeze. However, it has been discovered that the plant also has more positive uses. The roots have been used to reduce fatigue and as a cure for toothache.

Yarrow is a common plant of short grassland, producing flat-topped clusters of almost 'grubby' white flowers on tall stems with dark, feathery leaves.

Sneezewort has attractive daisy-like flowers in branched clusters at about knee-height, and very narrow leaves.

Yarrow

Sneezewort

RANGE: Throughout Europe

FLOWERING TIME
June to September

RANGE: Throughout Europe

FLOWERING TIME
July to August

Ground Elder/Hoary Cress

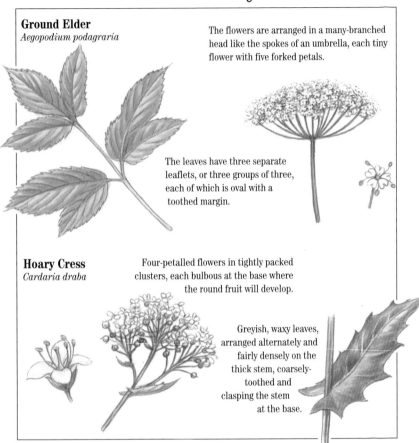

Ground Elder
Aegopodium podagraria

The flowers are arranged in a many-branched head like the spokes of an umbrella, each tiny flower with five forked petals.

The leaves have three separate leaflets, or three groups of three, each of which is oval with a toothed margin.

Hoary Cress
Cardaria draba

Four-petalled flowers in tightly packed clusters, each bulbous at the base where the round fruit will develop.

Greyish, waxy leaves, arranged alternately and fairly densely on the thick stem, coarsely-toothed and clasping the stem at the base.

Woodland

Ground Elder is a plant feared by gardeners, for it is a persistent weed of shady places and woodland edges with highly invasive roots, the smallest fragment of which can give rise to a new colony. In former times it was encouraged to grow near human habitation, as the leaves could be eaten when cooked, and it was cultivated by monks as a cure for gout. In spite of its bad reputation, Ground Elder is nevertheless an attractive plant when in flower, with rounded clusters of white blooms held on stems just above the dense covering of mid-green leaves, which bear a resemblance to those of Elder.

Hoary Cress is a plant of waste-places and disturbed soils, with a particular liking for the verges of recently made roads and motorway verges. It has increased its spread north-wards in recent years from its native southern Europe. In early summer, great drifts of it occur which, once identified, are easily recognized by their greyish, frosted appearance and foams of white flowers; it never becomes very tall. The plant could easily be taken for a member of the carrot family, but close examination of the flowers show that they have four petals, and are not carried in an 'umbel' arrangement.

Rough wasteland

Ground Elder *colonizes shady areas with a dense covering of three-part leaves at about knee-height, and produces rounded heads of white flowers on taller stems.*

Hoary Cress *has a greyish appearance, producing frothy masses of white flowers on disturbed soils, so that from a distance the ground appears to be covered with foam.*

Ground Elder

RANGE: Throughout Europe, except the far North

FLOWERING TIME
May to July

Hoary Cress

RANGE: Throughout Europe, except much of Scandinavia and Ireland

FLOWERING TIME
May to June

73

Fool's Parsley/Wild Carrot

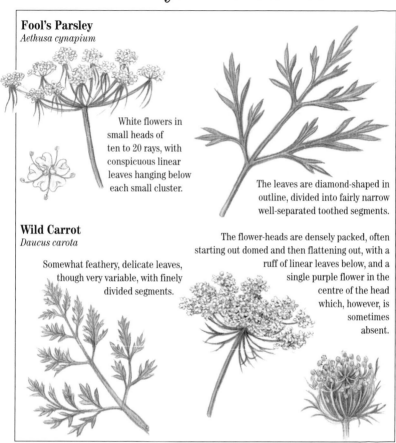

Fool's Parsley
Aethusa cynapium

White flowers in small heads of ten to 20 rays, with conspicuous linear leaves hanging below each small cluster.

The leaves are diamond-shaped in outline, divided into fairly narrow well-separated toothed segments.

Wild Carrot
Daucus carota

Somewhat feathery, delicate leaves, though very variable, with finely divided segments.

The flower-heads are densely packed, often starting out domed and then flattening out, with a ruff of linear leaves below, and a single purple flower in the centre of the head which, however, is sometimes absent.

Farmland

These two species and those on the next few pages belong to the carrot family, in which all members have groups of small flowers at the end of a set of branches which radiate from a single point, like the spokes of a wheel or umbrella. Recognizing each species can be difficult, as the leaves and the flower-heads often look similar, but there are usually one or two determining factors. With **Fool's Parsley** it is the thin thread-like nature of the leaves called bracteoles which droop down below each small cluster of flowers. This plant is extremely poisonous, and is commonest in arable fields, farmyards and gardens. However, the toxins disappear when the plant is dried, and so it is harmless in a crop of hay.

Wild Carrot has a ruff of thread-like leaves below the flower-head, but its most conspicuous feature is the one tiny purple flower right in the centre. As the fruits develop, the ruff of leaves curl upward and dry, so that the whole has the appearance of a little bird's nest. This plant is the origin of the cultivated carrot, but the root of the wild plant bears little resemblance to the vegetable. It grows in almost any dry, open grassy situation, including coasts.

Grassy meadows

74

Fool's Parsley *is a rather short plant of cultivated land, usually no more than knee-high, with a spreading and delicate appearance, smallish flower-heads and lace-like leaves.*

Wild Carrot *is a very variable plant of dry open grassland, from ankle- to waist-height, but quite robust in stature. It is usually not very leafy but the flower-heads are always densely-packed.*

Fool's Parsley

RANGE: Throughout Europe, except the extreme North and South

FLOWERING TIME
June to October

Wild Carrot

RANGE: Throughout Europe, except much of Scandinavia

FLOWERING TIME
June to August

Cow Parsley/Upright Hedge-parsley

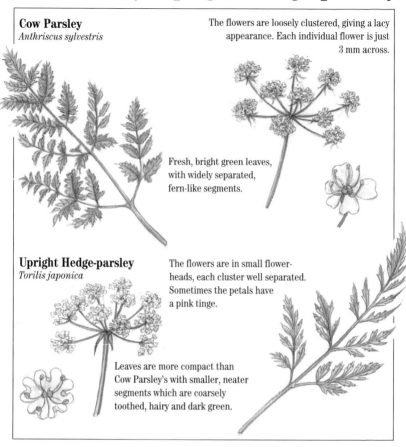

Cow Parsley
Anthriscus sylvestris

The flowers are loosely clustered, giving a lacy appearance. Each individual flower is just 3 mm across.

Fresh, bright green leaves, with widely separated, fern-like segments.

Upright Hedge-parsley
Torilis japonica

The flowers are in small flower-heads, each cluster well separated. Sometimes the petals have a pink tinge.

Leaves are more compact than Cow Parsley's with smaller, neater segments which are coarsely toothed, hairy and dark green.

Both species: hedgerows, roadsides

Swathes of tall white flowers along roadsides and through open woods in May are likely to be **Cow Parsley**. They appear like great waves of foam, and are a sign that spring is well and truly established. The leaves often appear as early as December in mild climates, and a few plants may flower earlier than the mass showing which is so familiar. A similar plant of damp places in the uplands and the North is Sweet Cicely (*Myrrhis odorata*), which has finer fern-like leaves, large long seed-pods and a sweet aniseed fragrance.

Upright Hedge-parsley is a similar plant to Cow Parsley growing in similar situations: the chief difference is that it comes into flower at least two months later. It is also a finer plant, with fewer and smaller flower-heads, and smaller, darker green leaves. There is often a tiny leaf at the base of the main flower stalk. Another similar plant whose flowering time occurs between the two is Rough Chervil (*Chaerophyllum temulentum*), but this has hairy, red spotted stems. Although some of these plants have edible leaves when young there are many fatally poisonous species with which they could be confused, so they are best avoided.

Cow Parsley produces masses of frothy white flowers along roadsides in spring, usually waist- to shoulder-high and with an open, spreading habit.

Upright Hedge-parsley is shorter and more delicate, not more than waist-high, with fewer leaves and smaller flower-heads so that the whole plant is much less substantial.

Cow Parsley

RANGE: Throughout Europe

FLOWERING TIME
April to June

Upright Hedge-parsley

RANGE: Throughout Europe, except the far North

FLOWERING TIME
July to September

Hogweed/Wild Angelica

Hogweed
Heracleum sphondylium

The seed is flattened from side to side like an oval disc. About 8 mm long.

Broad, flat flower-heads, about 150 mm across, with the outer petals noticeably larger than the inner ones.

The leaves are coarsely lobed into usually five large, hairy, dark green toothed leaflets, often becoming blackish, with a sheath at the base of the stalk.

The leaves are twice-divided into neat, oval, finely-toothed leaflets, the upper ones having a very large inflated sheath at the base.

Wild Angelica
Angelica sylvestris

Pinkish white domed flower-heads, which may be up to 150 mm across, on reddish-brown stems.

Hedgerows, roadsides

These are both tall, broad-leaved members of the carrot family which flower in midsummer. Though variable, **Hogweed** is a coarse, hairy plant with large lobed leaves and an unpleasant smell, and is common everywhere on roadsides and wasteground, particularly where the soil has been disturbed. The broad, flat heads have rather large flowers, whose petals are larger on the outside of the head than the inside, and these often provide a platform for hundreds of nectar-seeking insects in late summer. The sap can be irritating to the skin, but that of Giant Hogweed (*Heracleum mantegazzianum*), which can grow to an astonishing 4 m tall, can cause severe blisters.

    Wild Angelica prefers moist sites such as riversides, marshes and reedbeds. It, too, has broad leaves and stout stems, but these are often coloured reddish, sometimes strongly so, and the broad, domed flower-heads have a pink tinge. The upper leaves have large, inflated sheaths at their bases, so the emerging flower-buds look as though they are held in a cup. The plant has a sweet smell like that of Garden Angelica (*Angelica archangelica*), which has green flower-heads and whose candied stems are used in cake decoration.

Marshland

Hogweed *is a robust and rather unattractive plant, of waist- to head-height or taller, with rough-looking stems and leaves and a generally coarse appearance.*

Wild Angelica *is just as stout and robust but is somehow 'better-dressed' and more refined, with its compact flower-heads and smoother red stems like sticks of rock-candy.*

Hogweed

Wild Angelica

RANGE: Throughout Europe, except the far North

FLOWERING TIME
June to September

RANGE: Throughout Europe

FLOWERING TIME
July to September

79

Hemlock

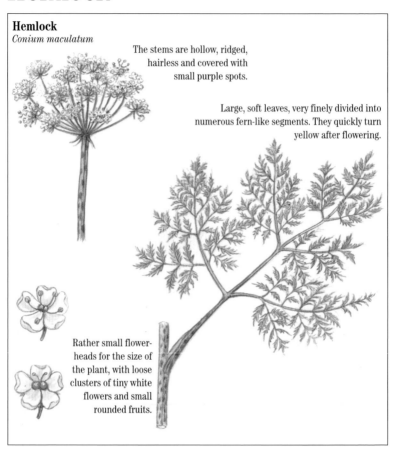

Hemlock
Conium maculatum

The stems are hollow, ridged, hairless and covered with small purple spots.

Large, soft leaves, very finely divided into numerous fern-like segments. They quickly turn yellow after flowering.

Rather small flower-heads for the size of the plant, with loose clusters of tiny white flowers and small rounded fruits.

Hedgerows, roadsides

A tall, imposing plant, up to 2 m high, often forming large colonies on riversides, damp wasteground and more recently the ditches and embankments that line newly constructed roads. Famously it was the poison administered to Socrates at his execution. All parts of the plant are extremely toxic: they contain the chemical coniine, which even in minute quantities is fatal to most animals. It causes paralysis of the entire body, including the respiratory system, so that the victim dies of asphyxia even though the brain remains alert to the end. Not surprisingly this property proved useful in early medicine, under closely controlled conditions, as a sedative and muscle relaxant but it is now considered too dangerous for medical use. Fortunately Hemlock is easily identified and cases of accidental poisoning are rare. It has very elegantly cut yellow-green, fern-like leaves, and characteristic smooth purple-spotted stems, as well as a strong disagreeable mousy odour, which should be enough to ward off even the most adventurous of diners. The scientific name *Conium* comes from the Greek *konas*, which means to whirl about – a reference to the sensation of vertigo suffered by the victim in the early stages of poisoning.

80

Hemlock usually forms large colonies, taller than a man, but the delicate fern-like leaves and small flower-heads give it an airy and delicate look, accentuated by its pale green or yellowish colour. Its rigid, hollow stems are a distinctive feature, blotched with purple spots. The seeds of Hemlock should be avoided as they are the most poisonous part of the plant.

Hemlock

RANGE: Throughout Europe,
except for northern Scandinavia

FLOWERING TIME
Flowers for a short period in June to July

81

Common Valerian/Dwarf Elder

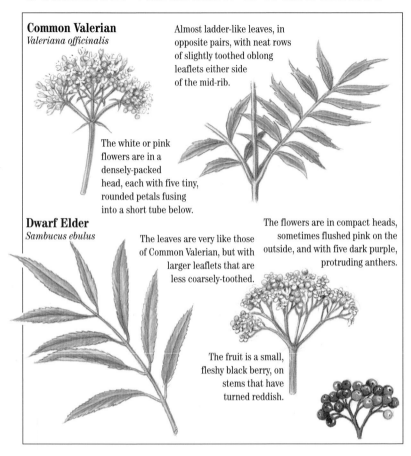

Common Valerian
Valeriana officinalis

Almost ladder-like leaves, in opposite pairs, with neat rows of slightly toothed oblong leaflets either side of the mid-rib.

The white or pink flowers are in a densely-packed head, each with five tiny, rounded petals fusing into a short tube below.

Dwarf Elder
Sambucus ebulus

The leaves are very like those of Common Valerian, but with larger leaflets that are less coarsely-toothed.

The flowers are in compact heads, sometimes flushed pink on the outside, and with five dark purple, protruding anthers.

The fruit is a small, fleshy black berry, on stems that have turned reddish.

Grassy meadows

Common Valerian can easily be mistaken for a member of the carrot family with its domed heads of densely packed flowers and divided leaves, but the flowers do not arise from a single point. It inhabits meadows, woodland margins and other undisturbed sites with rich vegetation, often rising up high among other tall vegetation to show off its delightful white or pale pink flowers. These have a distinctive odour that some find unpleasant. Preparations of the plant have been used for centuries as a sedative. It is also peculiarly attractive to cats, which find it irresistible if grown in the garden.

Dwarf Elder grows in similar situations, particularly on uncut road verges, though with a more southerly distribution. It is like an herbaceous form of the Elder shrub, though with larger leaflets and flat heads of small white flowers, which are pink in bud and have conspicuous purple anthers. These later form juicy black berries which are not as edible as those of the shrub, but the whole plant, including the roots, has a variety of medical uses. It is a persistent perennial, often reappearing in the same place for many decades, or even centuries.

Hedgerows, roadsides

***Common Valerian** is an attractive and neat plant of waist- to shoulder-height, whose delicate flower-heads are often held proudly above other lush vegetation.*

***Dwarf Elder** is a much more robust plant, inclined to form dense patches of about chest-height and whose large leaves are recognizable even at a distance.*

Common Valerian

RANGE: Throughout Europe, except the far North

FLOWERING TIME
June to August

Dwarf Elder

RANGE: South of Scandinavia and north of Britain

FLOWERING TIME
July to August

Water-plantain/Flowering rush

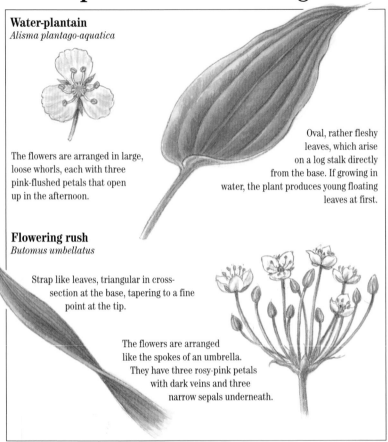

Water-plantain
Alisma plantago-aquatica

The flowers are arranged in large, loose whorls, each with three pink-flushed petals that open up in the afternoon.

Oval, rather fleshy leaves, which arise on a log stalk directly from the base. If growing in water, the plant produces young floating leaves at first.

Flowering rush
Butomus umbellatus

Strap like leaves, triangular in cross-section at the base, tapering to a fine point at the tip.

The flowers are arranged like the spokes of an umbrella. They have three rosy-pink petals with dark veins and three narrow sepals underneath.

Both species: ponds, ditches

Water-plantain is more easily noticed for its leaves than its flowers. They rise up through the water, or directly from the muddy edge of a pond or ditch, thick, fleshy and a simple oval in shape, with a curve that has been described by artists as exhibiting perfect proportion.

The flower-stem rises high above the leaves, with whorls of smaller stalks in tiers, decreasing in size towards the top. The flowers themselves are surprisingly small, with three petals tinged with the palest pink or lilac. They open in the afternoon, and each lasts only a day.

Flowering rush is an attractive plant of similar situations. It goes completely unnoticed until flowering time: the thin, narrow leaves, triangular in cross section, are just like those of true rushes and sedges with which it often grows. The flowers arise from a single point on a round stem, though on stalks of unequal length, and when in bud resemble the spokes of an upturned umbrella. Each of the flowers has three waxy petals which are pale pink with darker pink veins. The plant is becoming scarcer because of inappropriate dredging and 'tidying-up' of ditches and ponds.

Water-plantain makes a bold statement as it rises up out of the mud or water's edge with its large elliptical leaves, topped with thin flowering-stems like radio aerials on a building.

Flowering rush is almost invisible among other narrow-leaved plants until its pale pink flowers open out like an tiny inverted umbrella.

Water-plantain

RANGE: Throughout Europe, except for northern Britain and northern Scandinavia

FLOWERING TIME
June to August

Flowering rush

RANGE: Central and southern Europe, and south-eastern Britain.

FLOWERING TIME
Short period in July or August

Foxglove

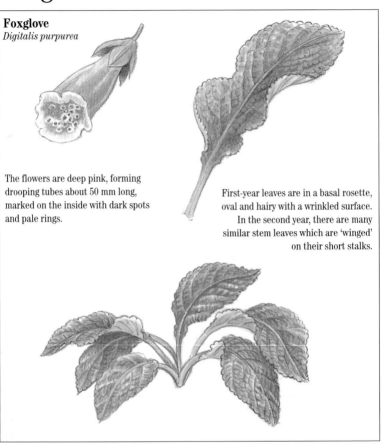

Foxglove
Digitalis purpurea

The flowers are deep pink, forming drooping tubes about 50 mm long, marked on the inside with dark spots and pale rings.

First-year leaves are in a basal rosette, oval and hairy with a wrinkled surface. In the second year, there are many similar stem leaves which are 'winged' on their short stalks.

Woodlands

The tall pink or crimson spires of Foxglove are a familiar sight in midsummer, but only where the soils are slightly acidic or rich in humus: it cannot cope with the alkaline conditions of chalk or limestone. It is immediately recognizable by its tiered ranks of pale purple bells drooping down one side of the tall stems. The bells are much loved by bumble bees which, when not pollinating them, seek shelter inside them from the rain. The leaves are easily recognized even when the flowers are not present in the first year of life, for they are large, wrinkled and hairy, though not so downy as those of its cousin, Great Mullein. It is an extremely poisonous plant, containing the chemical digitalin, which strengthens the beat of the heart. It is all too easy to administer an overdose and stop the heart altogether, but studies of the effects of Foxglove in the 18th century marked the beginnings of modern pharmacology. Heart-stimulating drugs are still prepared today from related Foxglove species. In spite of its toxic properties the plant has found favour with gardeners in various colour forms, and these occasionally escape into the countryside. In its natural state, it occurs in open woodland, embankments and roadsides.

86

Foxglove may form extensive colonies on disturbed acidic soils, often in the company of bracken fern, when its tall columns of flowers appear like a view of distant church spires rising above a city.

Foxglove

RANGE: Throughout Europe, except the extreme north-east

FLOWERING TIME
June to September

Common Centaury/Herb Robert

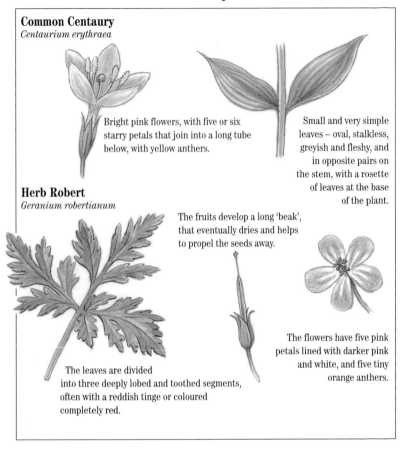

Common Centaury
Centaurium erythraea

Bright pink flowers, with five or six starry petals that join into a long tube below, with yellow anthers.

Small and very simple leaves – oval, stalkless, greyish and fleshy, and in opposite pairs on the stem, with a rosette of leaves at the base of the plant.

Herb Robert
Geranium robertianum

The fruits develop a long 'beak', that eventually dries and helps to propel the seeds away.

The flowers have five pink petals lined with darker pink and white, and five tiny orange anthers.

The leaves are divided into three deeply lobed and toothed segments, often with a reddish tinge or coloured completely red.

Grassy meadows

Common Centaury is a delightful plant of dry grassland, often on slopes, because it dislikes wet soils. The bright pink flowers are sometimes seen in great profusion, and at first sight appear to be simple five or six-petalled stars, but close examination shows that each petal joins together to form a long tube beneath. A member of the gentian family, it was greatly revered for its bitter properties as a tonic for the digestive system. It is named from the Centaur Chiron of Greek mythology, who supposedly used the plant to cure himself of a poisoned arrow wound.

Herb Robert is a very common geranium often associated with human habitation or wherever there are old walls or embankments, as well as in woodland rides and clearings. It is rarely regarded as a pest however, for its cheerful pink flowers with dark and light radiating lines brighten up many a dull corner of the garden. The leaves, too, are often enhanced with a red tinge, in fact sometimes the whole leaf may be completely scarlet. At other times, the flowers may be white. The visual appeal of the plant is not matched by its fragrance, which is distinctly mousy.

Woodland

Common Centaury's *bright pastel pink flowers shine out like little stars among the dull greens and yellows of dry grassland and are impossible to miss.*

Herb Robert *hides its flowers more carefully, often dotted about sporadically among a wealth of leaves, necessary for the more shady situations that it inhabits.*

Common Centaury

RANGE: Most of Europe, avoiding northern Britain and Scandinavia

FLOWERING TIME
June to September

Herb Robert

RANGE: Throughout Europe, except the extreme North

FLOWERING TIME
May to September

89

Dove's-foot Crane's-bill/Common Stork's-bill

Dove's-foot Crane's-bill
Geranium molle

The flower has five, deeply-notched, pink petals, with faint radiating lines.

Common Stork's-bill
Erodium cicutarium

The rounded or kidney-shaped leaf is lobed and gently toothed, and covered with soft hairs.

The long-beaked fruit releases seeds from its base, remaining attached by a long, spirally-twisted tail or filament.

Flowers vary in size and colour, from white to deep pink, but often have two petals very slightly larger than the others.

The leaves are feathery or fern-like in appearance, with rows of deeply-cut leaflets either side.

Farmland

Dove's-foot Crane's-bill is a delicate plant with the long flowering period typical of an annual that grows from fresh seed every year. It follows that it needs some bare soil in which to germinate, and so is often found on cultivated- and wasteground, as well as in gardens. The rounded leaves are covered with fine hairs and are extremely soft to the touch. They are lobed or cut to about half way, and the pink petals of the flowers are similarly notched so that there appears to be ten of them, when in fact there are five.

Common Stork's-bill is a related plant whose fruit has a very long 'beak'. Each seed is attached to this beak by a long filament, but as the fruit develops, the filament coils up into a spiral. When the seeds are expelled and exposed to moist ground, the filament straightens again and helps to 'drill' the seed into the soil. The flowers vary in colour widely from white to deep pink, but often begin to lose their petals at midday in sunny weather. The plant prefers dry grassy and bare places, often on sandy soils.

Heathland

Dove's-foot Crane's-bill *is usually no more than ankle-high, with tiny pink flowers that peep out shyly from the leaves, which look soft to the touch even at a distance.*

Common Stork's-bill *often sprawls over sand at ankle-height in an untidy jumble of angled stems and fruits, though may grow to knee-height if among tall grass.*

Dove's-foot Crane's-bill

RANGE: Throughout Europe, except much of Scandinavia

FLOWERING TIME
April to October

Common Stork's-bill

RANGE: Throughout Europe

FLOWERING TIME
May to September

91

Red Campion/Ragged Robin

Red Campion
Silene dioica

The leaves form a basal tuft at first, spear-shaped on long stalks and rather hairy. Upper leaves are oval, stalkless and in opposite pairs on the stem.

The flowers have five rose or deep pink, slightly notched petals, with a tube of red sepals beneath. Male and female flowers are on separate plants.

Ragged Robin
Lychnis flos-cuculi

The flowers have five petals divided into long, narrow lobes (untidy appearance), and with dark-striped reddish sepals below.

Leaves in opposite pairs, narrow and pointed, though wider at the base of the plant.

Woodland

Red Campion is the perfect complement to the white flowers of Stitchwort and the blue of Bluebells in springtime woods and hedgerows, or occasionally on coastal cliffs. Although the leaves are relatively simple – oval or shaped like the blade of a spear and covered with fine hair – they are immediately recognizable in little tufts along woodland rides just as winter gives way to spring. The scientific name *dioica* refers to male and female flowers existing on different plants, though without very close examination they look almost identical. The name is used for many other plants with the same characteristic.

Ragged Robin is the marsh-loving cousin of Red Campion, usually growing among tall grasses and spending part of the year with a shallow layer of fresh water over its roots. The flowers have an unkempt appearance, caused by each petal being neatly lobed into four narrow segments, which become caught up with one another. It is sadly becoming scarcer as wet meadows are drained for agricultural purposes: its presence is an indicator of an ancient meadow still in good condition.

Marshland

Red Campion usually grows up to waist-height and produces many loosely scattered pink flowers, but in profusion when the plant is growing in full sunlight.

Ragged Robin is generally more difficult to spot. The deeply-cut flowers are less showy at a distance and the plant is often hidden by tall marshland vegetation.

Red Campion

RANGE: Throughout Europe, though sometimes local

FLOWERING TIME
May to June

Ragged Robin

RANGE: Throughout Europe

FLOWERING TIME
May to June

Soapwort/Water Avens

Soapwort
Saponaria officinalis

Flowers in tight clusters, each with five pale pink, narrow petals rather like the fins of an aircraft propeller, and a long green sepal tube below.

Leaves in opposite pairs, pale green and waxy with veins.

Water Avens
Geum rivale

The leaves have large toothed lobes either side, with small lobes in between.

Pendent flowers, a few together in a loose cluster, with pinkish petals and dark red sepals enclosing many anthers.

It is thought that **Soapwort** probably originated in the Middle East, but it has been established in Europe for so many centuries that it is difficult to be certain. It was introduced for its extraordinary ability to produce a soap-like substance – saponin – which gives the leaves

Hedgerows, roadsides a greasy feel when rubbed between the fingers – and which produces a froth of lather if the leaves are boiled. The plant is often found near human habitation, or semi-shady places such as woodland edges and hedgebanks. It was associated with the textile industry as it is excellent for cleaning fabrics, and is still used today for the careful treatment of historical artefacts such as tapestries.

Water Avens is an unusual member of the rose family that occurs in wet shady meadows and marshes or in wet woodland. It is easily overlooked, unless growing *en masse,* for the small flowers nod down shyly, and the pale orange-pink petals are almost obscured by the deep red sepals. The fruit is bolder, with its stems that become erect to display a collection of spiky seeds with hooked bristles. The plant is related to Wood Avens, and when they occur together hybrids are formed.

Woodland

94

Soapwort *is a dazzling plant of knee- to waist-height with its bright clusters of bold pink flowers, which show up brightly in the shade of a hedgerow.*

Water Avens *is a rather shy and insignificant plant by contrast, no more than knee-high. The nodding flowers may be partially hidden, though the large, lobed leaves are distinctive.*

Soapwort

Water Avens

RANGE: Throughout Europe, except northern Scandinavia and northern Britain

RANGE: Throughout Europe

FLOWERING TIME
June to September

FLOWERING TIME
May to September

Crow Garlic/Thrift

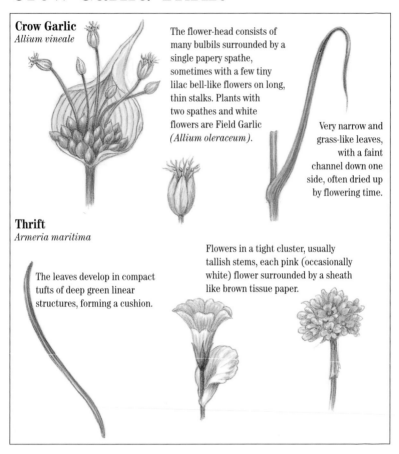

Crow Garlic
Allium vineale

The flower-head consists of many bulbils surrounded by a single papery spathe, sometimes with a few tiny lilac bell-like flowers on long, thin stalks. Plants with two spathes and white flowers are Field Garlic (*Allium oleraceum*).

Very narrow and grass-like leaves, with a faint channel down one side, often dried up by flowering time.

Thrift
Armeria maritima

Flowers in a tight cluster, usually tallish stems, each pink (occasionally white) flower surrounded by a sheath like brown tissue paper.

The leaves develop in compact tufts of deep green linear structures, forming a cushion.

Grasslands

Crow Garlic is difficult to spot when growing among tall grass, especially when just the leaves are present. Once the flower-head arrives, the plant is more noticeable — looking like bulbs of garlic on long sticks. A single papery spathe surrounds the flower-head, which consists of many green or red teardrop-shaped bulbils, each of which may form a new plant and which sometimes start to grow while still attached to the parent. In some cases true flowers are produced on thin hair-like stems. If growing in cattle pasture the plant imparts an onion flavour to milk.

Thrift is a plant of seaside cliffs and grassy beaches, and sometimes grows in such profusion that it colours whole areas pink. It is rather variable in height, depending on grazing pressure and local conditions. Thrift is becoming a familiar garden plant with many cultivated varieties available, but nothing beats the sight of wild thrift on a cliff-top lawn. The plant also occurs inland near old lead mines, or where the soil has a high lead content, which explains the scientific name of its family – *Plumbaginaceae* – from the Latin *plumbus*, for lead.

Coast

Crow Garlic looks like an over-sized hat-pin on its long, thin stalk, often up to waist-high, difficult to spot among tall grass but forming a mini-forest in short grass by the seaside.

Thrift forms expanses of bright pink cushions on the coast, which can be seen at considerable distance or high up on cliff ledges, with each flower-head like a pink lollipop growing out of a nest of thread-like leaves.

Crow Garlic	Thrift

RANGE: Throughout Europe, except northern parts of Britain and Scandinavia

FLOWERING TIME
June to August

RANGE: Coasts, except the Mediterranean, where similar species occur

FLOWERING TIME
April to August

Common Knapweed/Greater Knapweed

Common Knapweed
Centaurea nigra

Flower-heads made up of hundreds of reddish-purple rays, with a hard, knobbly globe below covered by feathery bracts with a triangular central section.

Long, and narrow or spear-shaped leaves, with a pale central vein, and sometimes slightly lobed or toothed. They are rather hairy and the stems are very tough and fibrous.

Greater Knapweed
Centaurea scabiosa

The leaves are large, and divided into narrow, toothed lobes either side.

Flower-heads are up to 50 mm across, with spreading outer branched florets. The bracts have a dark horseshoe-shaped section, and long feathery bristles.

Both species: grassy meadows

When the flowers of **Common Knapweed** begin to open in the grassy meadows and on roadsides, take it as proof that summer has arrived. At first glance, the plant bears a close resemblance to a thistle, but there are no spines, and underneath the purplish-red brush-like flowers are a set of curiously shaped bracts. In this species, these have a black triangular section with feathery bristles on either side. Occasionally, a form occurs with branched outer ray florets, superficially like those of Greater Knapweed. In some parts of Europe, Brown Knapweed *(Centaurea jacea)* is more common than Common Knapweed, with a papery brown fringe to the bracts.

　　Greater Knapweed is a more showy plant than Common Knapweed, with larger flower-heads and leaves which are much more deeply-divided into narrow lobes, rather like those of Field Scabious, from which it borrows its scientific name. It has a ring of long outer florets which branch at the tips, giving it a rather elegant appearance. Its bracts are larger, with a horseshoe-shaped feathery fringe. It, too, occurs on road verges and dry grassland, but always on limestone or chalky soils.

Common Knapweed *often creates extensive colonies in meadows, with thousands of black and pinkish-purple flower-heads waving on stiff stems just above the grass, at about knee-height.*

Greater Knapweed *is usually taller and more imposing, to about waist-height, and is apt to form clumps of more showy, reddish-purple flowers.*

Common Knapweed

RANGE: In Britain, western France, the Netherlands and southern Scandinavia

FLOWERING TIME
June to September

Greater Knapweed

RANGE: Throughout Europe, except for northern parts of Britain and Scandinavia

FLOWERING TIME
July to September

Greater Burdock/Marsh Thistle

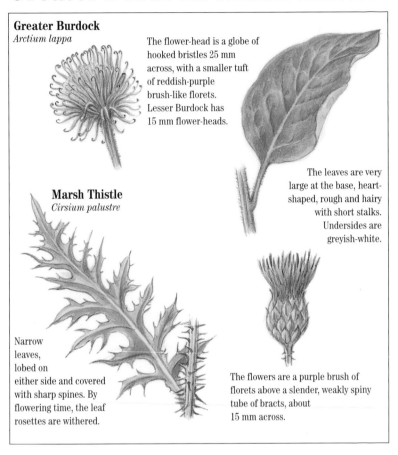

Greater Burdock
Arctium lappa

The flower-head is a globe of hooked bristles 25 mm across, with a smaller tuft of reddish-purple brush-like florets. Lesser Burdock has 15 mm flower-heads.

The leaves are very large at the base, heart-shaped, rough and hairy with short stalks. Undersides are greyish-white.

Marsh Thistle
Cirsium palustre

Narrow leaves, lobed on either side and covered with sharp spines. By flowering time, the leaf rosettes are withered.

The flowers are a purple brush of florets above a slender, weakly spiny tube of bracts, about 15 mm across.

Rough wasteland

Greater Burdock is an extremely robust plant that is difficult to miss, for the leaves can be 50 cm long or more. It is rough and hairy, found on roadsides, wasteland and woodland edges, and is famous for its burs – spiny, hooked flower-heads that attach themselves to clothing with amazing ease. Plenty, though, stay attached to the plant to be scattered around as it springs back to its original position after being disturbed by a passer-by. The roots are an antidote for a wide range of medical complaints, and can be combined with Dandelion root to produce a refreshing drink. Lesser Burdock is a similar plant with smaller flowers.

Marsh Thistle is a very tall, slender plant of damp meadows, marshes and woodland margins. It starts as a flat rosette of leaves covered with needle-like dark spines, but in its second year the single, thin stem can grow to almost two metres, seemingly too slender to support the plant, and is completely covered with small spiny wings. The flower-heads, too, are surprisingly small, so that the whole plant has a very characteristic appearance.

Marshland

Greater Burdock *is a stout and vigorous plant growing to shoulder-height on the edges of fields, often with enormous leaves at the base and topped with spreading clusters of its globular, spiny flowers.*

Marsh Thistle *grows even taller, often over head-height, but is thin and lanky in comparison with its erect stems and tight little cluster of rather small flower-heads at the top.*

Greater Burdock

RANGE: Throughout Europe, except northern Britain and Scandinavia

FLOWERING TIME
July to September

Marsh Thistle

RANGE: Throughout Europe, except the extreme north

FLOWERING TIME
July to September

Creeping Thistle/Spear Thistle

Creeping Thistle
Cirsium arvense

The flower-heads
have spineless
bracts below, and a
small ruff of usually
mauve florets, about
20 mm across.

The leaves are rather small and less
rigid than other thistle species,
but have a spiny margin. The
underside has a
cottonish texture. The
stems are slender,
without spines.

Spear Thistle
Cirsium vulgare

Stiff, strongly lobed leaves,
with very sharp spines, on
stems completely covered
with spiny wings.

Flower-heads are an almost spherical
ball of bracts, about 30 mm across,
covered with sharp, stiff spines which are wooly
at the base, topped with a spreading array of
pinkish-purple flowers (see far right).

Farmland

Creeping Thistle is a most unwelcome plant for the farmer. Once it becomes established in rough pastures it is extremely difficult to eradicate, and spreads by means of creeping stems or runners, as well as the production of thousands of fluffy seeds. Any disturbed soil nearby such as roadsides, riverbanks or arable fields quickly become infested. It is usually not as tall as other thistles and has thin spineless stems, but very spiny leaves. The flowers are pale lilac or mauve and the seeds have distinctive grey-brown hairs which enable them to float easily on the wind.

Spear Thistle is a more robust plant with perhaps the sharpest spines of all the thistles. The leaves end in a long spear-shaped prickle, and the stems are covered with spiny wings. The flower-heads are highly attractive, with bold pinkish-red florets bursting out from the flask-shaped collection of bracts beneath, each of which ends in a sharp, yellow spine. Like Creeping Thistle this plant is a serious farmland pest, preferring disturbed, rich soils. It is almost certainly this species which was adopted as the national emblem of Scotland, symbolizing qualities which the Scots felt that they shared.

Creeping Thistle may form very large colonies, at about waist-height, and is easily recognizable by the masses of small but distinctively coloured flower-heads, which are more lilac or mauve than other thistles.

Spear Thistle may also be very numerous, but always as separate plants which are rather majestic and stately in appearance and with large, attractive flower-heads.

Creeping Thistle

RANGE: Throughout Europe, except the far North

FLOWERING TIME
June to September

Spear Thistle

RANGE: Throughout Europe, except the far North

FLOWERING TIME
July to October

Red Clover

Red Clover
Trifolium pratense

The flowers are rather variable in colour from pink to deep red, with many individual flowers densely packed into a rounded flower-head, cupped by a leaf immediately below.

The leaves have three rather narrow, elliptical leaflets, each with a pale chevron mark.

Grassy meadows

A meadow covered with the bright pink flowers of Red Clover in early summer is an uplifting sight, though sadly becoming scarcer. It may be an indicator of an old meadow managed by mowing and grazing for many decades: if not managed in this way, the clover and other wild flowers become crowded out by more robust grasses. Red Clover has also been used as a fodder crop, when it also nourishes soil by adding nitrogen compounds through the action of bacteria in the roots. Plants of this type are often taller, with paler flowers than the true wild form.

Red Clover is much loved by bumble bees, whose long tongues are able to reach down into the flowers for nectar. In some areas, the decline of old clover meadows has been matched by a decline in bumble bee species, and is becoming a serious cause for concern to conservationists.

Zigzag Clover (*Trifolium medium*) is a very similar species, also on the decline: its flower-heads lack the leaf immediately below, as there is in Red Clover.

Crimson Clover (*Trifolium incarnatum*) is another fodder crop species, with much longer, darker flower-heads.

Red Clover carpets old meadows with its red or deep pink rounded flower-heads, usually at ankle-height but growing taller where the grass is long. It is a prolific plant, flowering in grassy places, which nourishes the soil with nitrogen.

Red Clover

RANGE: Throughout Europe

FLOWERING TIME
May to June, and then sporadically until September.

Restharrow/Sainfoin

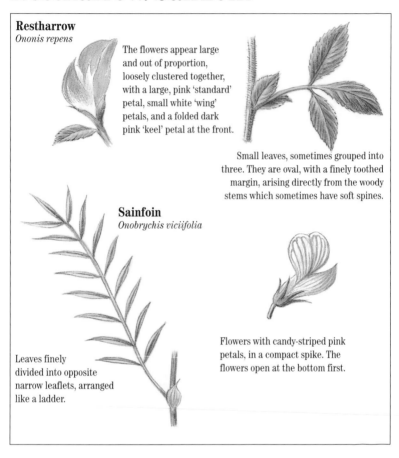

Restharrow
Ononis repens

The flowers appear large and out of proportion, loosely clustered together, with a large, pink 'standard' petal, small white 'wing' petals, and a folded dark pink 'keel' petal at the front.

Small leaves, sometimes grouped into three. They are oval, with a finely toothed margin, arising directly from the woody stems which sometimes have soft spines.

Sainfoin
Onobrychis viciifolia

Flowers with candy-striped pink petals, in a compact spike. The flowers open at the bottom first.

Leaves finely divided into opposite narrow leaflets, arranged like a ladder.

Both species: grassy meadows

Restharrow is a low, almost slightly shrubby member of the pea family found in grassy pastures, meadows and roadsides. It spreads over the ground, but underneath the soil it has a long, matted, extremely tough root system that could stop a horse-drawn plough dead in its tracks.

The plant has declined from arable fields since the arrival of mechanized tractors. It is said to be a favourite food of the donkey, and its scientific name comes from a Greek word for that animal – *onos*.

Sainfoin is also a plant with an agricultural background: it used to be planted as a fodder crop, and is today sometimes sown on newly-made road verges.

These plants tend to grow rather tall, with large spikes of flowers, while the true wild form grows short on pastures over limestone, hugging the ground and producing more compact spikes, though the flowers are just as beautiful, with delicately striped pink petals. It is unlikely to be confused with any other pea family-members – however the distinctive ladder-like leaves help to confirm identification. Its unusual, rounded seed-pods are also distinctive.

Restharrow *is a rather short and bushy plant, untidy in appearance as it creeps among the grass between ankle- and knee-height, and with its pretty flowers somewhat loosely arranged.*

Sainfoin *is very attractive, ankle- or knee-high irrespective of surrounding vegetation. The flowers are neatly clustered into cone-shaped spikes.*

Restharrow

RANGE: Western Europe and southern Scandinavia

FLOWERING TIME
June to September

Sainfoin

RANGE: Southern and central Europe, and southern Britain

FLOWERING TIME
June to September

Common Vetch

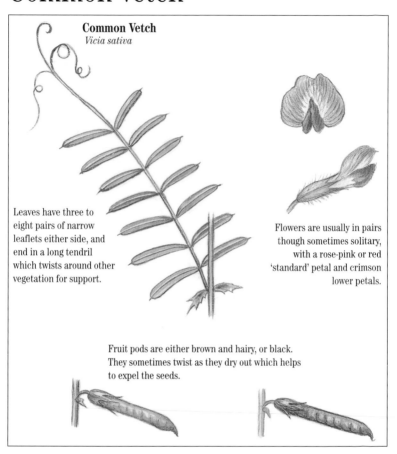

Common Vetch
Vicia sativa

Leaves have three to eight pairs of narrow leaflets either side, and end in a long tendril which twists around other vegetation for support.

Flowers are usually in pairs though sometimes solitary, with a rose-pink or red 'standard' petal and crimson lower petals.

Fruit pods are either brown and hairy, or black. They sometimes twist as they dry out which helps to expel the seeds.

Grassy meadows

Common Vetch is one of the prettiest and certainly one of the most common members of the pea family, found on roadsides, woodland edges, wasteground and grassy places everywhere. The deep rich red of the flowers, sometimes edging towards crimson or purple, is set off perfectly by the foil of bright green leaves. In common with many other pea plants, which include the vetches, it was used as a fodder crop for cattle, but the use of such crops decreased dramatically in the first half of the 20th century with the advent of chemical fertilizers, often with a corresponding decline in farmland wildlife. One of Common Vetch's defining characters is the pair of stipules: small triangular leaf-like organs at the base of the leaves where they join the main stalk, which each carry a clear black dot in the centre. These are almost constantly visited by ants, a strategy which the plant no doubt employs in order to ward off other insect species; nevertheless the leaves frequently show some damage. The plant is very variable as a result of its use in cultivation, and has been divided into several 'subspecies', one of which has ripe fruit-pods which are shiny and black. Plants with pinker flowers and brown, hairy, ripe pods are more likely to be the truly wild form.

Common Vetch often scrambles among tall grasses up to waist-height, so that it goes unnoticed until seen close-by, when its brilliant crimson flowers shine out. It was introduced from southern Europe as a fodder crop for cattle and is now established throughout northern Europe.

Common Vetch

RANGE: Throughout Europe

FLOWERING TIME
May to September

Common Hemp-nettle/Black Horehound

Common Hemp-nettle
Galeopsis tetrahit

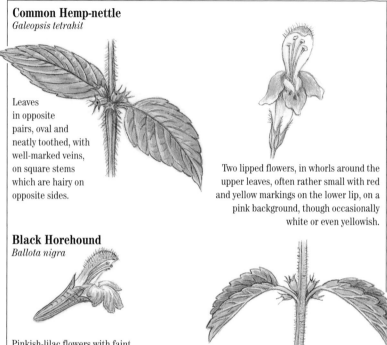

Leaves
in opposite
pairs, oval and
neatly toothed, with
well-marked veins,
on square stems
which are hairy on
opposite sides.

Two lipped flowers, in whorls around the
upper leaves, often rather small with red
and yellow markings on the lower lip, on a
pink background, though occasionally
white or even yellowish.

Black Horehound
Ballota nigra

Pinkish-lilac flowers with faint
markings on the lower lip, in a
dense whorl around the upper
leaves, each with a spiky salver-
shaped sepal tube.

Oval, coarsely toothed
leaves, usually rather dark green, producing
an offensive smell if rubbed.

Common Hemp-nettle distinguishes itself among the mint family
(along with Yellow Archangel and White Dead-nettle), by having a
neat and orderly appearance. It is an annual that prefers some disturbed
soil in which to germinate, and used to be common in arable fields, but

Hedgerows, roadsides now is just as likely in waste-places, woodland clearings, ditches and
river banks. Its scientific name *Galeopsis* means weasel-faced, as the flowers are supposed
to resemble a weasel. In fact, the flowers are variable, sometimes being mostly white or
yellow, but still with the same markings on the lower lip.

Black Horehound, by contrast, is always messy looking: unkempt and rough, with
spiky sepal tubes which turn blackish-brown as the nutlets within start to ripen, and
generally has a 'dirty' appearance. It also carries an unpleasant
smell, and is rejected by cattle as a result, indeed the scientific name
Ballota comes from the Greek for rejection. The plant occurs in
equally scruffy places, on waste- and disturbed-ground, alongside
paths and roads, sometimes in the shade, and often associates with
the Stinging Nettle.

Rough wasteland

Common Hemp-nettle
*has a soft, gentle
appearance, with
neatly arranged leaves
and understated
flowers, usually about
knee-high, and is
easily passed by
without being noticed.*

Black Horehound *is a
waist-high scruffy
plant of scruffy places,
often dirty looking,
rough to the touch,
and the smell is not
too good, either.*

Common Hemp-nettle

RANGE: Throughout Europe

FLOWERING TIME
April to June

Black Horehound

RANGE: Throughout Europe, except northern
parts of Scandinavia and Britain

FLOWERING TIME
June to September

Wild Basil/Betony

Wild Basil
Clinopodium vulgare

Two-lipped flowers, plain pink and with few markings, arranged in a downy whorl above the upper leaves.

The leaves are oval and in opposite pairs, hairy and with a very slightly toothed margin.

Betony
Stachys officinalis

Very distinctive leaves – dark green with neat rounded teeth – a little like an oak leaf. They often droop down from the flower clusters.

The flowers are in tight whorls at the top of the plant, mostly without leaves in between. Pink or reddish-purple, with an upright upper lip.

Both species: grassy meadows

Wild Basil is a pretty though shy plant of dry grassland and heaths in midsummer. Unlike many of its close relatives in the mint family, it has only a faint scent and is not related to any of the culinary herbs. The name *Clinopodium* means foot of the bed – a fanciful reference to the tufted whorls of flowers supposedly resembling the knobs on an old-fashioned bedstead. It is a softly hairy plant that often only produces a few flowers at a time, but is nonetheless very attractive.

Betony has been greatly revered by herbalists for many centuries. It is closely related to the woundworts, but this species was considered to be the most efficacious as a panacea for a wide range of ailments. Its properties became legendary, such that wounded animals were believed to seek it out, or that two snakes placed within a ring of it would fight each other to the death. Its healing abilities are not unfounded, and a tea made from the leaves is an effective cure for headache. It grows in undisturbed grassy places on a variety of soils and is most easily recognized by the characteristically drooping oval leaves which are wrinkled, with rounded teeth, somewhat resembling an oak leaf.

Wild Basil *has a delicate look about it, not very leafy but displaying its few bright pink flowers proudly on slender stems below knee-height.*

Betony *is also delicate and somewhat straggly, about the same height as Wild Basil, but with the leaves neatly arranged.*

Wild Basil

RANGE: Throughout Europe, except northern Scandinavia and Ireland

FLOWERING TIME
July to September

Betony

RANGE: Throughout Europe, except the North and Scandinavia

FLOWERING TIME
June to September

Red Dead-nettle

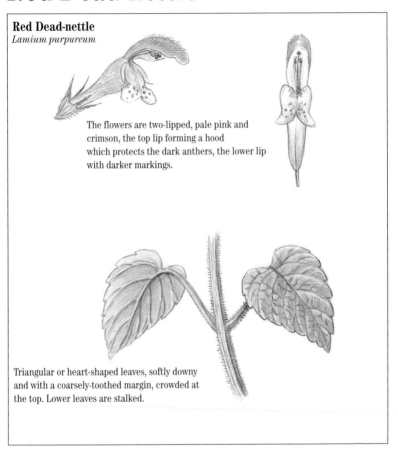

Red Dead-nettle
Lamium purpureum

The flowers are two-lipped, pale pink and
crimson, the top lip forming a hood
which protects the dark anthers, the lower lip
with darker markings.

Triangular or heart-shaped leaves, softly downy
and with a coarsely-toothed margin, crowded at
the top. Lower leaves are stalked.

Rough wasteland

Red Dead-nettle is an ubiquitous plant, which starts afresh every
year from seed wherever there is some bare ground to
accommodate it, making it common on wasteground or arable fields,
in scrappy corners by sunny walls and in freshly dug gardens. In fact,
it is so familiar that it almost goes unnoticed.

The heart-shaped leaves are often crowded very close together, especially towards
the top of the plant, and the pink two-lipped flowers seem to squeeze their way
through the mass of foliage.

When this happens, the leaves seem to take on something of the colour of the
petals, and become progressively tinged with red towards the top. If growing amongst
other tall vegetation, however, the plant is forced to extend itself to reach the light,
and in these circumstances the leaves remain green.

It is a favourite of bees, and as the flowers are smaller than those of its close
relatives, even short-tongued species may take the nectar which is presented so early
in the year: the plant is often in flower as early as February, and specimens may still
be found as late as November, where climatic conditions allow.

Red Dead-nettle always has its red-tinged upper leaves crowded together, and often forms small ankle-high patches on rough ground. It is one of the earliest plants to flower in the year. A member of the mint family, this plant does not sting as it is not related to the Common Nettle.

Red Dead-nettle

RANGE: Throughout Europe, except the far North

FLOWERING TIME
February to December

Water mint/Wild Marjoram

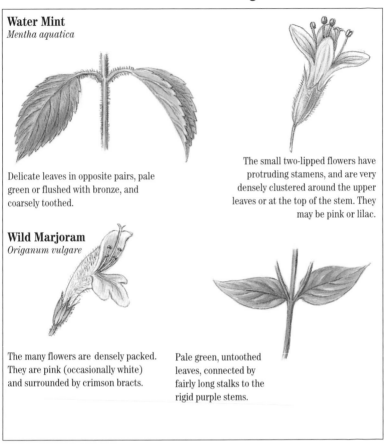

Water Mint
Mentha aquatica

Delicate leaves in opposite pairs, pale green or flushed with bronze, and coarsely toothed.

The small two-lipped flowers have protruding stamens, and are very densely clustered around the upper leaves or at the top of the stem. They may be pink or lilac.

Wild Marjoram
Origanum vulgare

The many flowers are densely packed. They are pink (occasionally white) and surrounded by crimson bracts.

Pale green, untoothed leaves, connected by fairly long stalks to the rigid purple stems.

Marshland

O n hot, sunny days the air is refreshed in marshy meadows by the sweet scent of **Water Mint**, but if the leaves are picked and crushed in the hand the fragrance is over-powerful, almost sickly. The plant grows luxuriantly wherever the ground is permanently moist, in swamps and the margins of rivers and ditches. It may grow tall in lush waterside conditions, and can be recognized by the domed clusters of flowers at the top of the plant, which vary between pink or distinctly lilac, in which case the leaves take on a bronzy hue.

In some ways **Wild Marjoram** is rather similar, except that it only occurs on the driest grasslands and roadsides, usually on limestone or chalky soils. It produces wide, spreading sprays of pink flowers, each surrounded by deep crimson bracts, so that there is a colourful effect. It is the source of the culinary herb Oregano, and its smell is instantly recognizable if the leaves are rubbed, though in more northerly latitudes the fragrance is not so strong as that in the Mediterranean. It is a favourite with butterflies for its nectar, and in particular the day-flying burnet moths.

Grassy meadows

Water Mint is very distinctive, often up to knee-height with plenty of bushy growth and with clearly red-tinged leaves that release their fragrance as they are brushed past.

Wild Marjoram is also knee-high and bushy, but produces foaming masses of pink and crimson flowers in its dry grassland home.

Water Mint

Wild Marjoram

RANGE: Throughout Europe, except the far North

FLOWERING TIME
July to September

RANGE: Throughout Europe, except the far North

FLOWERING TIME
July to September

117

Wild Thyme

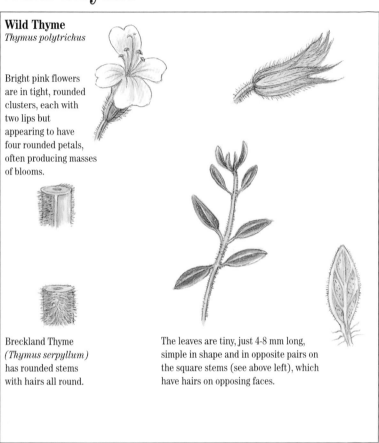

Wild Thyme
Thymus polytrichus

Bright pink flowers are in tight, rounded clusters, each with two lips but appearing to have four rounded petals, often producing masses of blooms.

Breckland Thyme
(Thymus serpyllum) has rounded stems with hairs all round.

The leaves are tiny, just 4-8 mm long, simple in shape and in opposite pairs on the square stems (see above left), which have hairs on opposing faces.

Grassy meadows

This species of thyme keeps close to the ground and prefers well-drained turf in sunny situations, on either chalky or sandy soils or even on shingle. The thyme we associate with the kitchen garden is another species, *Thymus vulgaris*, which originates in the Mediterranean region and is a more bushy plant with upright stems, though there are many other varieties available with citrus-like scents or variegated leaves. The flowers are much loved by bees, and in some areas they produce excellent honey. The plant's low, creeping habit means that it is easily trodden on and this makes it release its characteristic, refreshing fragrance, long-esteemed for its purifying properties. Wild Thyme was often a component of the posy, originally a device to protect from infectious diseases, and the plant does contain a high proportion of thymol, a powerful antiseptic. The leaves used to be made into an infusion and drunk as prevention against nightmares and preparations were even sold in shops as a cure for headaches and coughs. In eastern and northern Europe this species is replaced by the almost identical Breckland Thyme (*Thymus serpyllum*), which has rounded stems rather than square, and with a fine covering of hairs all the way round, though a hand-lens is needed to see them.

Wild Thyme forms low cushions among short turf on dry soils, difficult to spot when not in flower, but otherwise producing an abundance of clustered pink flowers. When the plant's leaves are crushed, the scent of thyme is released, although it is not the species grown for culinary use.

Wild Thyme

RANGE: Western and southern Europe

FLOWERING TIME
May to September

Common Lousewort/Red Bartsia

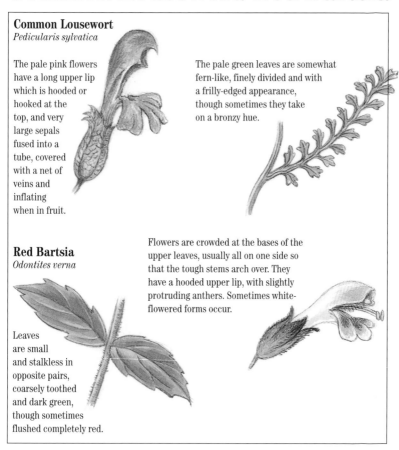

Common Lousewort
Pedicularis sylvatica

The pale pink flowers have a long upper lip which is hooded or hooked at the top, and very large sepals fused into a tube, covered with a net of veins and inflating when in fruit.

The pale green leaves are somewhat fern-like, finely divided and with a frilly-edged appearance, though sometimes they take on a bronzy hue.

Red Bartsia
Odontites verna

Flowers are crowded at the bases of the upper leaves, usually all on one side so that the tough stems arch over. They have a hooded upper lip, with slightly protruding anthers. Sometimes white-flowered forms occur.

Leaves are small and stalkless in opposite pairs, coarsely toothed and dark green, though sometimes flushed completely red.

Heathland

Common Lousewort is a plant of bogs, moors and heaths on acid soils and is similar in many ways, apart from the colour of its flowers, to Yellow-rattle (page 200). It, too, is a semi-parasite, deriving some of its nutrients directly from the roots of surrounding grasses, and it also produces inflated papery seed-pods. Its English name of Lousewort refers not to any ability to dispel lice, but to the belief that it spread lice to sheep: almost undoubtedly a myth, since sickness in sheep is almost certainly due to the marshy conditions in which they graze.

Red Bartsia has flowers which in many ways are similar to Common Lousewort's, but the whole plant has a very different appearance. It grows typically on roadsides and tracks through meadows or in the gateways to pastures, wherever the soil is regularly disturbed or trampled. Often the whole plant becomes tinged with a deep crimson, so that a colony appears like little tufts of rusty wire poking up from the ground. Downy hairs cover the surfaces of the stems and leaves, making for a dusty look; however, the plant's situation often means that it is simply covered in dust.

Grassy meadows

Common Lousewort *is usually a low tufted plant, often producing flowers directly from the base so that the slender pink petals seem to be arranged in a nest of frilly leaves.*

Red Bartsia *has tough wiry stems, sometimes arching over and sometimes branched like a candelabra, generally between ankle- and knee-height.*

Common Lousewort

RANGE: Throughout Europe, except the far North

FLOWERING TIME
May to July

Red Bartsia

RANGE: Not in southern Ireland and northern Scandinavia

FLOWERING TIME
June to September

Redshank/Amphibious Bistort

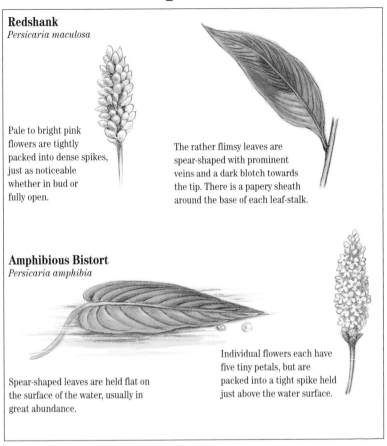

Redshank
Persicaria maculosa

Pale to bright pink flowers are tightly packed into dense spikes, just as noticeable whether in bud or fully open.

The rather flimsy leaves are spear-shaped with prominent veins and a dark blotch towards the tip. There is a papery sheath around the base of each leaf-stalk.

Amphibious Bistort
Persicaria amphibia

Spear-shaped leaves are held flat on the surface of the water, usually in great abundance.

Individual flowers each have five tiny petals, but are packed into a tight spike held just above the water surface.

Rough wasteland

Redshank is one of those ubiquitous weeds that can be overlooked because it is so familiar. Nonetheless, its short columns of bright pink flowers are an attractive sight in the derelict waste-places in which it often grows, usually on bare or recently disturbed soil in damp areas; it is frequently seen on building sites before the surrounding land becomes tidied up. The dark blotch on the surface of each leaf is a useful diagnostic feature. Pale Persicaria (*Persicaria lapithifolia*), is very similar, but has greenish-white flowers and no dark leaf-blotch.

Amphibious Bistort is Redshank's aquatic relative, usually seen as pale pink spikes of flowers held just above the surfaces of ponds, lakes or slow-moving rivers and streams. It is common where the water has a high nutrient content, perhaps as a result of run-off from nearby farmland. It is also seen in fresh water fishing lakes, where it is ignored by hungry carp and its floating leaves need not struggle for light in the muddy water. Sometimes a land-dwelling form is produced in the muddy edges of ponds or cultivated fields. It looks similar to Redshank, but usually has shorter stems.

Ponds, ditches

122

Redshank *forms ragged patches of branching stems up to knee-height with short scattered spikes of flower-heads.*

Amphibious Bistort *often creates extensive mats of leaves on the water surface, dotted with attractive spikes of pink flowers, like an aquatic colony of orchids.*

Redshank

RANGE: Throughout Europe

FLOWERING TIME
June to October

Amphibious Bistort

RANGE: Throughout Europe, except
northern Scandinavia

FLOWERING TIME
June to September

Heather

Heather
Calluna vulgaris

The leaves are like tiny scales
in opposite pairs. They overlap
one another almost like the
shoots of a moss.

The flowers are just 3 mm long, drooping
down from densely-packed, long conical
spires. Pink, pale purple, lilac and
occasionally white forms are produced.

This is a familiar plant of dry sandy soils, which when left to itself also grows as a straggly plant in the clearings and rides of open woodland. But it is better known as the staple inhabitant of wide-open heathlands and moors, which were created by man by clearing trees to provide low-grade grazing pasture. The plant was an invaluable resource for peasant communities: its springy, woody branches were used to stuff mattresses; to thatch roofs; to strengthen primitive mud-and-clay walls; and it was made into household articles such as brooms and rope. The abundance of the flowers and the sweetness of their nectar make it a favourite of beekeepers, and the flowering tops have been used for making beer, a practice recently revived on a commercial scale in Scotland. The young shoots are surprisingly soft and palatable, and provide food for game birds such as grouse. Where grouse are nurtured for sport, the young growth is stimulated by cutting or burning the plant. Heather is unmistakable in late summer when its tiny lilac or pink flowers are open, and entire hillsides may be saturated with their colour. Its flowers and leaves, which are like tiny overlapping scales, are much smaller than those of other heather (*Erica*) species.

Heathland

124

Heather forms springy clumps from ankle- to waist-height, which are straggly and woody at the base. It is often in huge colonies, colouring the landscape when in flower. Although it grows slowly, it lives a long time. The tiny leaves, in pairs on small branches, are leathery, becoming rough to the touch as they mature.

Heather

RANGE: Throughout Europe

FLOWERING TIME
July to September

Early Purple Orchid/Fragrant Orchid

Early Purple Orchid
Orchis mascula

The leaves, all in a basal rosette, are long and narrow, glossy green with dark purple-brown blotches.

The flowers are purple, with narrow upper petals often drooping down. The lower lip is folded back somewhat. A pale patch in the centre is speckled with tiny black dots.

Fragrant Orchid
Gymnadenia conopsea

Leaves sprout mostly from the base of the plant. They are plain green, very narrow and slightly folded along their length.

Pale lilac-pink or (rarely) white flowers, with a lower lip that has three rounded lobes, and a long curving 'spur' drooping down behind.

Woodlands

In springtime woods, just before the leaves of trees begin to open, the leaf rosettes of **Early Purple Orchid** can be seen among the bluebells and other plants, strikingly blotched with dark brown patches. It also occurs in meadows and grasslands on chalky soils. The scientific name Orchis comes from the Greek for testicle: a reference to the plant's two rounded tubers carried below ground – they were thought to possess aphrodisiac qualities; they have also been used to make a sweet drink which has its origins in the Middle East.

Fragrant Orchid occurs on dry grassy sites, usually on slopes, although it may sometimes be found in damp areas. In common with other orchid species, the number of blooms varies from year to year, and sometimes hundreds of its pale lilac-pink spikes can be seen. Each flower has a remarkably long 'spur' holding the nectar, which can only be reached by long-tongued insects. They are attracted by its faint, clove-like scent, which becomes more powerful in the evening as the moths awake from their daytime slumber.

Grassy meadows

Early Purple Orchid *produces a proud spike of deep purple flowers, easily seen even in the semi-shade of woodland. They nestle in a cup of heavily spotted leaves.*

Fragrant Orchid *spikes are just as noticeable as those of Early Purple Orchid, but the individual flowers are small and dainty, giving the plant a more delicate look than many similar orchid species.*

Early Purple Orchid

RANGE: Throughout Europe, except most of Scandinavia

FLOWERING TIME
April or May

Fragrant Orchid

RANGE: Throughout Europe, though rare in Denmark and the Netherlands

FLOWERING TIME
June or July

Common Spotted Orchid/Heath Spotted Orchid

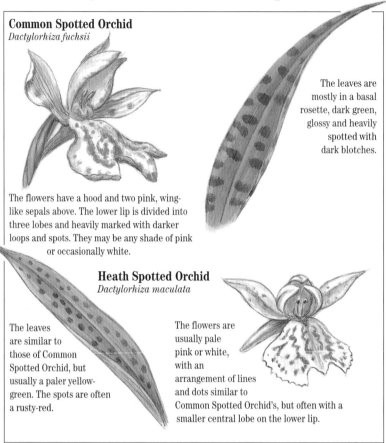

Common Spotted Orchid
Dactylorhiza fuchsii

The leaves are mostly in a basal rosette, dark green, glossy and heavily spotted with dark blotches.

The flowers have a hood and two pink, wing-like sepals above. The lower lip is divided into three lobes and heavily marked with darker loops and spots. They may be any shade of pink or occasionally white.

Heath Spotted Orchid
Dactylorhiza maculata

The leaves are similar to those of Common Spotted Orchid, but usually a paler yellow-green. The spots are often a rusty-red.

The flowers are usually pale pink or white, with an arrangement of lines and dots similar to Common Spotted Orchid's, but often with a smaller central lobe on the lower lip.

Grassy meadows

These two orchids are almost different versions of the same plant, each preferring different soil conditions. The **Common Spotted Orchid** lives in a wide range of grassy sites such as meadows, woodland edges and even waste tips, but always where the soil is chalky or alkaline in nature. The scientific name *Dactylorhiza* means 'finger-root', a reference to the finger-like tubers hidden from view. There are many other orchid species with this scientific name, all with pink or purple flowers in a similar arrangement. They hybridize freely with each other, which can make identification very difficult, and sometimes the best guide is the geographic location in which the plant is found. The two species here are the commonest and most widely distributed members of this group.

Heath Spotted Orchid is like the pale flowered form of Common Spotted Orchid, but grows in acidic soils such as bogs and heaths and is the more prolific of the two where these conditions prevail. Why they have such conspicuously spotted leaves is a mystery, for they offer no advantageous camouflage, nor do they warn of a poisonous nature, for the leaves are relished by grazing animals.

Heathland

__Common Spotted Orchid__ produces striking pink blooms in midsummer, often in considerable quantity, usually between ankle- and knee-height.

__Heath Spotted Orchid__ has flower-heads which are usually paler than Common Spotted Orchid's, and which show up brightly against the dark soils and deep green of heathland vegetation.

Common Spotted Orchid

RANGE: Europe, except most of Scandinavia, Belgium and Holland

FLOWERING TIME
June or July

Heath Spotted Orchid

RANGE: Throughout Europe

FLOWERING TIME
June or July

Pyramidal Orchid

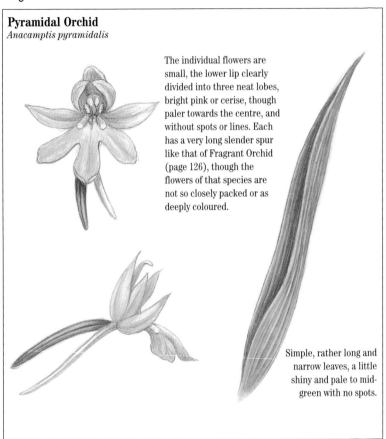

Pyramidal Orchid
Anacamptis pyramidalis

The individual flowers are small, the lower lip clearly divided into three neat lobes, bright pink or cerise, though paler towards the centre, and without spots or lines. Each has a very long slender spur like that of Fragrant Orchid (page 126), though the flowers of that species are not so closely packed or as deeply coloured.

Simple, rather long and narrow leaves, a little shiny and pale to mid-green with no spots.

Grassy meadows

Pyramidal Orchids are perhaps the easiest orchids of all to recognize, for although the colour varies a little, they are always a very bright, and sometimes an extremely intense pink, so they can be easily spotted growing along the roadside. They are often the first orchid species to colonize new grassland such as reclaimed farmland, road verges or even roundabouts, and may sometimes appear in their hundreds. The scientific name *pyramidalis* refers to the shape of the flower-head which forms a distinct cone, but only when in bud, for once all the flowers have opened a more cylindrical shape is assumed. Many orchid species in Europe prefer long-established, undisturbed sites, and may take years to reach flowering maturity. The seeds of orchids are extremely tiny, like dust, contain almost no nutrient of their own and so must form an association with a microscopic fungus in the soil in order for the plant to grow. This fungus lives inside the roots of the orchid and provides its essential nutrition during the first growth stages. The orchid is able to capitalize on this and may not flower or even appear above ground for some years. Some species have even become wholly dependant on the fungus, deriving all their nutrition from it and producing no chlorophyll with which to manufacture their own food.

Pyramidal Orchid is difficult to miss, with its cones or pyramids of shocking pink blooms in midsummer. It varies in size from ankle- to knee-high depending on the local growing conditions, though always on calcareous soils.

Pyramidal Orchid

RANGE: Central and southern Europe, avoiding Scotland, Scandinavia and northern areas

FLOWERING TIME
June to July

Bee Orchid/Late Spider Orchid

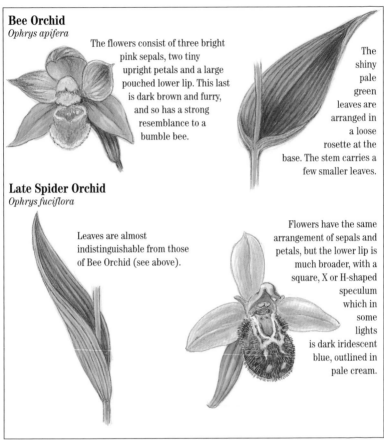

Bee Orchid
Ophrys apifera

The flowers consist of three bright pink sepals, two tiny upright petals and a large pouched lower lip. This last is dark brown and furry, and so has a strong resemblance to a bumble bee.

The shiny pale green leaves are arranged in a loose rosette at the base. The stem carries a few smaller leaves.

Late Spider Orchid
Ophrys fuciflora

Leaves are almost indistinguishable from those of Bee Orchid (see above).

Flowers have the same arrangement of sepals and petals, but the lower lip is much broader, with a square, X or H-shaped speculum which in some lights is dark iridescent blue, outlined in pale cream.

Both species: grassy meadows

Bee Orchids have a curiously-shaped and relatively large flower which seems out of proportion to the short single stem and rather insignificant leaves. There are many other *Ophrys* species in southern Europe with similarly elaborate flowers, and these are visited by male bees which, mistaking the flower for a female bee, attempt to mate with it and so effect pollination. The Bee Orchid, however, has evolved self-pollination as an effective method of reproduction and sets ample seed without the amorous attentions of insects. It is found on dry grassy banks, roadsides and old meadows on chalky soils.

Late Spider Orchid at first sight appears rather similar to the Bee Orchid, but the lower lip is splayed out like an apron, with a small, green upturned tooth in the middle, and a patch more or less in the shape of the letter 'H' of dark shiny, almost metallic blue which is called the speculum. It occurs in the same habitats, but although it is long-lived it is intolerant of tall grasses and may easily disappear if regular grazing or mowing is not maintained. The Early Spider Orchid (*Ophrys sphegodes*) is very similar but has green sepals above the lip instead of pink ones.

Bee Orchid *may be partially hidden among taller grasses, but is so distinctive that it is easily spotted when one knows what to look for.*

Late Spider Orchids *look very similar to Bee Orchids but are more likely to be seen among shorter grasses, especially on road verges.*

Bee Orchid

Late Spider Orchid

RANGE: Western and southern Europe

FLOWERING TIME
May and June

RANGE: Sporadically across central and southern europe

FLOWERING TIME
June and July

Butterbur/Tree Mallow

Butterbur
Petasites hybridus

The flowers are dusty pink and tightly-packed into small heads, with many heads collected together into a cone-shape on a rather fleshy stalk.

The leaves all arise from the base, and are broadly kidney-shaped with a wrinkled edge. They continue to grow throughout the spring until they are as wide as a metre.

Tree Mallow
Lavatera arborea

More or less rounded leaves, with wrinkled lobes and a wavy margin; covered with soft downy hairs, particularly beneath.

Typical mallow type flowers, with a pale pink cone of anthers in the centre. The petals are a deep magenta-pink, though black at the base and with dark lines radiating outwards.

Ponds, ditches

Butterbur, once seen, is never forgotten. Its curious cones of pinkish -white flowers emerge from the ground close to streams or ditches, often in shady corners, but in late winter/early spring not many walkers are around to see it, especially if conditions are wet. Male and female flowers appear on different plants, but in many areas only the female flowers are produced and the plant spreads vegetatively. The leaves appear after the flowers, but grow to huge proportions, and their pliable nature makes them ideal for purposes such as makeshift hats, or for wrapping food – for example butter.

Tree Mallow is also very distinctive, forming a tall, woody shrub whose reddish bark is often scarred, with snakeskin-like scales where leaves were once attached. It always grows close to the sea, on shingle or rough ground just inland, or high up on cliff ledges. Its attractive appearance has made it a favourite of seaside gardeners, so you may get the impression that it has escaped from cultivation into the wild rather than the other way around. The densely hairy, velvety leaves – an adaptation against desiccation in the dry soils of its habitat – have been used as a soothing poultice for sprains.

Coast

Butterbur pushes up its conical spikes of pinkish flowers in early spring. They look something like ankle-high pink Christmas trees, and appear along damp streamsides.

Tree Mallow has the look of a garden Hibiscus, often shoulder-high or more, that has taken up residence on seaside shingle. The colour of the flowers seems almost too intense to be natural.

Butterbur

RANGE: Most of Europe, except the north of Britain and Scandinavia

FLOWERING TIME
March to April

Tree Mallow

RANGE: Southern and western coastal areas

FLOWERING TIME
June to September

135

Common Mallow/Musk Mallow

Common Mallow
Malva sylvestris

The flowers have five well-separated deep pink petals, each with a distinct notch and radiating lines of mauve or magenta.

More or less kidney-shaped leaves, wavy or wrinkled and with shallow teeth on the margin.

Musk Mallow
Malva moschata

The lower leaves are more deeply toothed than those of Common Mallow. The upper leaves are divided into delicate, narrow lobes.

The flowers have less robust petals than Common Mallow and are a pale pink (occasionally white), with the faintest of sculpted lines.

Rough wasteland

Disturbed soils of wasteground, abandoned fields and the edges of cultivation are the habitat of **Common Mallow**. Its cheerful pink flowers appear in midsummer, and continue for several months, but as time goes on the soft leaves get eaten by insects and snails and the whole plant takes on a dishevelled and straggly appearance. The fruits are produced as a ring of nutlets joined together like the segments of an orange, but have also been likened to a miniature cheese and local names sometimes reflect this, especially as the nutlets are edible and enjoyed by children.

Musk Mallow is a prettier plant whose upper leaves are divided into filigree lobes. It is seen particularly on field edges and roadsides where there is shelter from a nearby hedge. The leaves and flowers have a musky scent, though this is slight and is best smelt by squeezing the leaves in the hand. Both these species are related to the much rarer Marsh Mallow (*Althaea officinalis*), a tall, pale-flowered plant of coastal marshes, whose leaves and roots carry a high percentage of mucilage, which has long been used to soothe inflammation, and formerly for making confectionary.

Hedgerows, roadsides

Common Mallow is often an untidy and scruffy plant of waist-height or thereabouts, but with neat flowers that look as though they were crafted in porcelain.

Musk Mallow is usually shorter, with a more elegant and refined appearance and whose delicate, sugary flowers are clustered together.

Common Mallow

RANGE: Throughout Europe, except much of Scandinavia

FLOWERING TIME
June to September

Musk Mallow

RANGE: Throughout Europe, except the far North

FLOWERING TIME
July to August

Rosebay Willowherb/Greater Willowherb

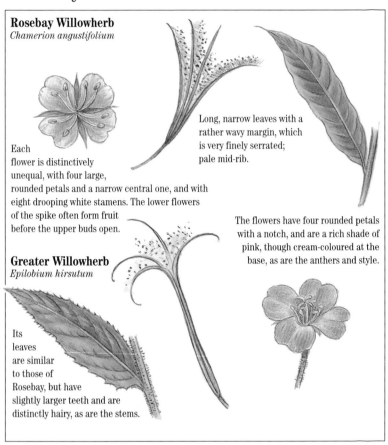

Rosebay Willowherb
Chamerion angustifolium

Each flower is distinctively unequal, with four large, rounded petals and a narrow central one, and with eight drooping white stamens. The lower flowers of the spike often form fruit before the upper buds open.

Long, narrow leaves with a rather wavy margin, which is very finely serrated; pale mid-rib.

The flowers have four rounded petals with a notch, and are a rich shade of pink, though cream-coloured at the base, as are the anthers and style.

Greater Willowherb
Epilobium hirsutum

Its leaves are similar to those of Rosebay, but have slightly larger teeth and are distinctly hairy, as are the stems.

Rough wasteland

Rosebay **Willowherb** has undertaken a remarkable transformation over the past hundred years or so: what was once a scarce plant of rocky places has now become common wherever man has brought stones to the surface of the soil, forming great colonies on railway embankments or building and industrial sites. It is often the first plant to appear after a devastating fire. As its flowering season progresses, the long silvery seed-pods split lengthways to expel vast numbers of fluffy seeds – up to 80,000 from one plant, which are carried on the wind to the next suitable site for this enterprising species to pioneer. Like Greater Willowherb, it can spread by means of long, creeping underground roots: a large colony may actually be a single plant with an extensive root system.

Greater Willowherb, by contrast, is a lover of damp places such as the edges of rivers and marshes or even moist roadside ditches, provided there is a little shelter to prevent this tall but fragile plant from being blown over. The leaves resemble those of the willow tree with which it often associates, but it may also be seen with Meadowsweet (page 68) or tall grasses such as Common Reed.

Marshland

Rosebay Willowherb *forms great drifts of head-high magenta-pink spires above lines of silvery seed-pods.*

Greater Willowherb *is just as tall as Rosebay Willowherb but it displays its flowers in a less regimented fashion. Although it, too, forms colonies, they are more likely to be mixed with other plants.*

Rosebay Willowherb

Greater Willowherb

RANGE: Throughout Europe

FLOWERING TIME
June to September

RANGE: Throughout Europe, except the far North

FLOWERING TIME
June to September

139

Hemp Agrimony/Orpine

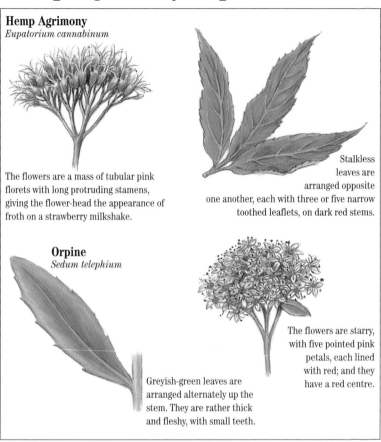

Hemp Agrimony
Eupatorium cannabinum

The flowers are a mass of tubular pink florets with long protruding stamens, giving the flower-head the appearance of froth on a strawberry milkshake.

Stalkless leaves are arranged opposite one another, each with three or five narrow toothed leaflets, on dark red stems.

Orpine
Sedum telephium

The flowers are starry, with five pointed pink petals, each lined with red; and they have a red centre.

Greyish-green leaves are arranged alternately up the stem. They are rather thick and fleshy, with small teeth.

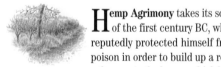

Hedgerows, roadsides

Hemp Agrimony takes its scientific name *Eupatorium* from a king of the first century BC, who was adept with herbal remedies and reputedly protected himself from poisoning by taking small doses of poison in order to build up a resistance. The name *cannabinum* is in reference to the leaves, which bear a resemblance to those of Cannabis, though it is unrelated. The flower-heads, much loved by butterflies and other insects, are a distinctive sight in late summer, usually seen in damp places such as the margins of rivers and marshes, though the plant may also appear on drier sites after tree clearance.

Orpine is a much shyer plant, preferring the semi-shade of hedge banks or mountain woods. It is a member of the stonecrop family, and its leaves and stems have the fleshy succulent character of those plants – indeed the plant is said to be able to stay fresh for many days if uprooted and hung up, living off the residual moisture in its tissues. Folklore has it that if two leaves, representing two lovers, are hung up together and one of them withers, then one of the unfortunate pair will die. The plant is closely related to the popular garden plant, *Sedum spectabile*.

Woodland

Hemp Agrimony
*makes shoulder-height
platforms of frothy
pink flower-heads in
late summer,
along roadsides.*

***Orpine** tends to hide
away at knee-height or
lower among other
vegetation such as
bracken, though the
vivid crimson of its
flowers is hard to miss
when close up.*

Hemp Agrimony

RANGE: Most of Europe,
except the far North

FLOWERING TIME
July to September

Orpine

RANGE: Most of Europe,
except the far North and most of Ireland

FLOWERING TIME
July to September

141

Bilberry/Scarlet Pimpernel

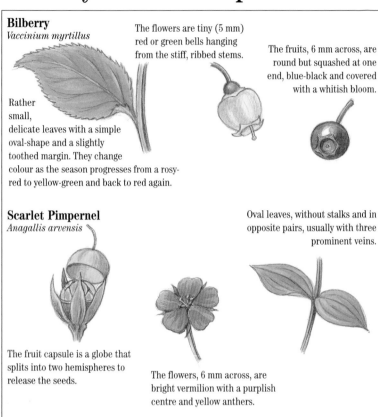

Bilberry
Vaccinium myrtillus

The flowers are tiny (5 mm) red or green bells hanging from the stiff, ribbed stems.

The fruits, 6 mm across, are round but squashed at one end, blue-black and covered with a whitish bloom.

Rather small, delicate leaves with a simple oval-shape and a slightly toothed margin. They change colour as the season progresses from a rosy-red to yellow-green and back to red again.

Scarlet Pimpernel
Anagallis arvensis

Oval leaves, without stalks and in opposite pairs, usually with three prominent veins.

The fruit capsule is a globe that splits into two hemispheres to release the seeds.

The flowers, 6 mm across, are bright vermilion with a purplish centre and yellow anthers.

Heathland

The fruits of the **Bilberry** are delicious, though their small size and haphazard distribution about the plant makes collecting them laborious: it must be done by hand, even if the berries are for commercial use. Though they are slightly sharp to the taste, they make an excellent jam when combined with a little sugar. The deep blue-black colour of the juice was used in the dyeing industry. This diminutive shrub prefers acid soils, and it may cover large areas of heaths and moors, particularly in the north and west or on mountains. It also occurs under the light shade of pine woods.

Provided that the sun is shining, **Scarlet Pimpernel** is impossible to pass by: the orange-vermilion flowers open wide and face upwards, though they may remain closed in dull weather. The flowers close automatically in the early afternoon, and then the plant seems to disappear from view as the leaves merge in with other vegetation. Sometimes, and particularly in southern Europe, a deep blue form occurs, though its flower still has the rich magenta-coloured centre. The plant occurs on arable or recently disturbed ground, but is a poor competitor with other plants, occupying its own patch of bare soil.

Farmland

Bilberry *may be easily dismissed as a low, knee-high shrubby plant of little interest, but it is worth looking below the leaves for the bell-like flowers.*

Scarlet Pimpernel *has brilliant red flowers that shine out brightly in good light, even though the plant hugs the surface of the ground.*

Bilberry

RANGE: Throughout Europe, but avoiding drier lowlands of France

FLOWERING TIME
April to June, fruit ripe in August

Scarlet Pimpernel

RANGE: Throughout Europe, except the far North

FLOWERING TIME
May to September

Common Poppy

Common Poppy
Papaver rhoeas

The flowers have four broad petals which overlap widely, and a black blotch at the base underneath the numerous black anthers.

The seed capsule is rather like a pepper pot, with holes around the rim from which the many seeds are shaken out by the wind.

Very hairy leaves, deeply divided into long, finger-like lobes. The stems and drooping flower-buds are also clothed in long hairs.

Farmland

The seeds of the Common Poppy may lie dormant in the ground for many years, but when they are brought to the surface, perhaps when a field has been ploughed more deeply than usual or after a period of neglect, then poppy flowers may be very abundant, seemingly outnumbering the crop that has been planted there. A similar effect was created by the wartime battlefields of Europe, and the poppy has come to represent the spilt blood of war's casualties. The tiny black seeds are used to decorate and add flavour to bread. There is little truth in the theory that they help to induce sleep in children, as this plant contains none of the morphine, narcotine and codeine found in the juice of the related Opium Poppy (*Papaver somniferum*), which usually has larger, pink or white flowers. If pressed, the seeds also yield an oil which was used in northern countries as a replacement for olive oil, and as a drying oil to mix with artists' oil paints (linseed oil is now used for this). In southern Europe, there are a few similar species of poppy, which have either elongated or bristly seed capsules, but they rarely occur in the same prodigious quantities. In the Mediterranean region, brightly coloured Anemones occur, typically in olive groves, which bear a superficial resemblance to poppies, but they have more than four petals.

Common Poppy forms a brilliant scarlet carpet in fields and cannot possibly be confused with anything else. Whole fields may be coloured bright red so that they may be seen from a great distance.

Common Poppy

RANGE: Throughout Europe,
except the extreme North and much of Finland

FLOWERING TIME
June to September

Salad Burnet/Common Fumitory

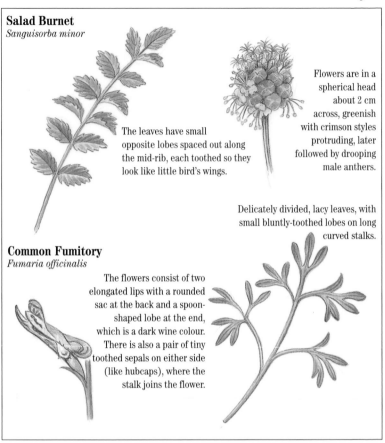

Salad Burnet
Sanguisorba minor

The leaves have small opposite lobes spaced out along the mid-rib, each toothed so they look like little bird's wings.

Flowers are in a spherical head about 2 cm across, greenish with crimson styles protruding, later followed by drooping male anthers.

Delicately divided, lacy leaves, with small bluntly-toothed lobes on long curved stalks.

Common Fumitory
Fumaria officinalis

The flowers consist of two elongated lips with a rounded sac at the back and a spoon-shaped lobe at the end, which is a dark wine colour. There is also a pair of tiny toothed sepals on either side (like hubcaps), where the stalk joins the flower.

Grassy meadows

Salad Burnet is an unlikely member of the rose family, but it is. The flowers are not immediately obvious, resembling little pom-poms on a short stalk. There are no petals as such, but when the bright red female styles burst out, then the landscape may be coloured by them, as the plant grows in profusion on dry grassland and rocky places with chalky soil. The styles are followed by the male yellow anthers, which droop down on thin filaments. The leaves have a faint scent of cucumber and can be added to salads, but are too bitter to eat in quantity. Greater Burnet (*Sanguisorba officinalis*) is a knee-high plant of damp meadows with larger (3-cm) oblong flower-heads that remain a deep claret colour.

Common Fumitory is found on the bare ground between crops in arable fields, though it sometimes occurs in pastures if the grass is not too vigorous. The filigree pattern of the leaves was seen to resemble the appearance of smoke at a distance, so the plant was given the name *Fumaria*, but this owes more than a little to the imagination of early botanists. There are several other similar species with slight variations in leaf shape and flower colour, but all have the notable arrangement of petals and spikes of radiating flowers.

Farmland

Salad Burnet grows usually little more than ankle-high, and may go unnoticed except for when the crimson styles open out on the flower-heads like little red lollipops.

Common Fumitory may be an abundant weed among arable crops, and though it, too, grows only to ankle-height, the deep red spiky looking flower-heads make it easy to notice.

Salad Burnet

RANGE: Europe except northern Scandinavia and Scotland

FLOWERING TIME
May to July

Common Fumitory

RANGE: Throughout Europe, but avoiding mountainous areas

FLOWERING TIME
May to October

Common Sorrel/Red Valerian

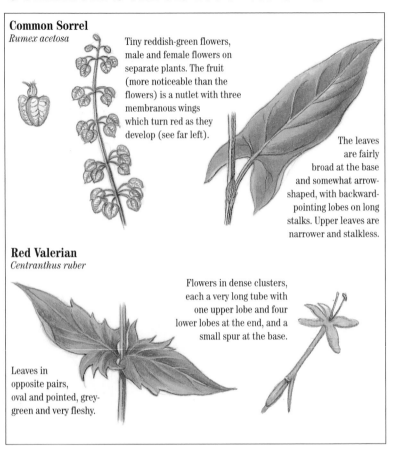

Common Sorrel
Rumex acetosa

Tiny reddish-green flowers, male and female flowers on separate plants. The fruit (more noticeable than the flowers) is a nutlet with three membranous wings which turn red as they develop (see far left).

The leaves are fairly broad at the base and somewhat arrow-shaped, with backward-pointing lobes on long stalks. Upper leaves are narrower and stalkless.

Red Valerian
Centranthus ruber

Flowers in dense clusters, each a very long tube with one upper lobe and four lower lobes at the end, and a small spur at the base.

Leaves in opposite pairs, oval and pointed, grey-green and very fleshy.

Grassy meadows

Common Sorrel is one of those ubiquitous plants frequently ignored precisely because it is so common. It looks like a weed, and its flowers are somewhat insignificant, but a meadow tinted scarlet by its thin, erect stems laden with fruit is a striking sight. They can be acid, and taste pleasantly sharp and thirst-quenching, so they make a useful addition to salads, soups and omelettes; or they can be cooked like spinach. It takes some time for the distinctive taste to develop in the leaves, and while most edible leaves of wild plants are best eaten when very young, in the case of Sorrel they should be left on the plant until the reddish fruit is mature, by which time the leaves are at their best.

Red Valerian is an attractive plant native to the Mediterranean, but introduced to northern Europe in the 16th century as a garden ornamental. Its habit of clinging to small ledges on cliffs, crevices in the walls of ruins and castles, and of growing on shingle beaches, has enabled it to spread easily into the wild and it undoubtedly adds to their charm. A deep magenta-pink is its most common colour, but deep crimson-red and white-flowered forms also occur; often all three are seen mixed together.

Rough wasteland

148

Common Sorrel *is an unprepossessing waist-high plant when viewed alone, but it transforms whole fields to a rich red colour when seen* en masse.

Red Valerian *is impossible to ignore, its foaming towers of deep pink, red or white flowers spilling out from walls and cliffs.*

Common Sorrel

RANGE: Throughout Europe

FLOWERING TIME
May and June

Red Valerian

RANGE: Around Mediterranean coasts, western France, Britain and Ireland

FLOWERING TIME
July to September

149

Wild Daffodil

Wild Daffodil
Narcissus pseudonarcissus

Leaves shaped like the blade of a sword, all arising from the base, sometimes slightly twisted.

The underground bulb is covered with a thin brown papery skin or tunic, and stores food to enable the plant to grow in early spring.

The flowers consist of a central bright yellow trumpet or corona, surrounded by six paler petals (properly called tepals), which are often slightly twisted. A papery spathe surrounds the flower when in bud.

Woodland

The vision of thousands of Wild Daffodils setting the woodland floor aglow in springtime is unforgettable, but it is becoming scarcer because the ash and oak woodland it favours often suffer from neglect, where once they were regularly managed by coppicing or grazing which allowed light to reach the ground. Once they were common at the boundaries of fields or in hedge banks, but they have declined here too. Although the brightly-coloured flowers have often been over-picked, even on a commercial scale, for decoration and as a symbol of the passing of winter into spring, this is unlikely to be the cause of their decline. The plant can grow year after year from its underground bulb in spite of picking, and long-term changes to its habitat such as ploughing of field edges and removing hedges is the real cause of its decline. In recent years there has been a fashion for planting cultivated varieties of daffodils in semi-wild situations such as remote road verges, and in some cases these have interbred with the wild form and so created hybrids which threaten the integrity of the truly wild species. The true Wild Daffodil, however grows shorter than many of its garden-bred cousins, and with its delicately two-toned flowers displays an exquisite beauty not shared by those gaudy impostors.

150

Wild Daffodil is instantly recognizable, with its bold central trumpet and ring of outer petals, but look for its small size and pale petals to separate it from the many garden varieties found in the wild. It forms colonies in ancient deciduous woodland and meadows, on river banks, and along hedgerows. The bulbs resemble onions, but should not be eaten as they are highly poisonous and can cause a fatal collapse of the nervous system.

Wild Daffodil

Range: Scattered locations in England and Wales, Ireland and western France and Spain

Flowering Time
March or April

Yellow Flag

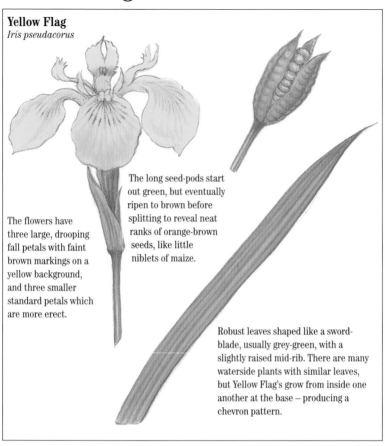

Yellow Flag
Iris pseudacorus

The flowers have three large, drooping fall petals with faint brown markings on a yellow background, and three smaller standard petals which are more erect.

The long seed-pods start out green, but eventually ripen to brown before splitting to reveal neat ranks of orange-brown seeds, like little niblets of maize.

Robust leaves shaped like a sword-blade, usually grey-green, with a slightly raised mid-rib. There are many waterside plants with similar leaves, but Yellow Flag's grow from inside one another at the base – producing a chevron pattern.

Ponds, ditches

Yellow Flag is the commonest iris growing in Europe, and the only bright yellow one. It is seen in all kinds of marshy areas: ponds, lakes and ditches, whether open or shady. The word Iris comes from the Greek name for the rainbow goddess, and is a reference to the many colours present in iris flowers, though blue usually dominates.

The roots yield a blue-black dye, whilst the flowers, not surprisingly, yield a yellow one. The dried root has also been used to treat toothache and cure obstinate coughs. It is the root of a related species, however, *Iris germanica* var. *florentina*, or Orris, which is held in highest esteem for its bitter properties and delicious violet scent. It grows in the Mediterranean region, particularly in Italy.

The seed-pods swell for many weeks, becoming remarkably heavy, drooping down almost like a ripe cocoa pod. In spite of their weight, when the pods eventually split open the expelled seeds float on the surface of water, which then carries them away to seed again elsewhere. When well roasted, the seeds were said to make an excellent substitute for coffee, or even to have a better flavour. However, the practise does not seem to have caught on. It is claimed that the seeds aid digestion.

Yellow Flag's bold flowers, at anything from waist- to shoulder-height, are unmistakeable when seen around a pond's edge, but the sword-like leaves are much harder to identify on their own. It often grows among other plant species with similar tall, sword-shaped leaves.

Yellow Flag

RANGE: Throughout Europe, except the north of Scandinavia

FLOWERING TIME
June to August

Biting Stonecrop/Common Rock-rose

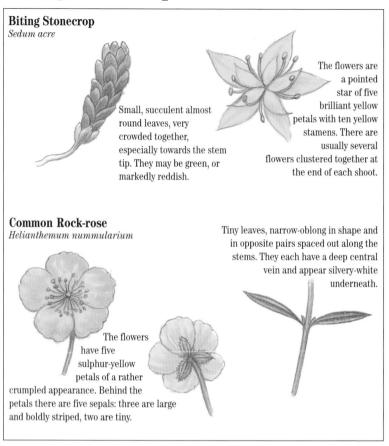

Biting Stonecrop
Sedum acre

Small, succulent almost round leaves, very crowded together, especially towards the stem tip. They may be green, or markedly reddish.

The flowers are a pointed star of five brilliant yellow petals with ten yellow stamens. There are usually several flowers clustered together at the end of each shoot.

Common Rock-rose
Helianthemum nummularium

Tiny leaves, narrow-oblong in shape and in opposite pairs spaced out along the stems. They each have a deep central vein and appear silvery-white underneath.

The flowers have five sulphur-yellow petals of a rather crumpled appearance. Behind the petals there are five sepals: three are large and boldly striped, two are tiny.

Coast

The tiniest cracks and crevices in old walls or on roofs are enough to give a foothold for **Biting Stonecrop**, though it is equally at home on shingle or other rocky places, and especially, though not always, near coasts. It can survive these inhospitably arid conditions by storing water in its little leaves, so they become fat and distended and the shoots take on the appearance of knobbly asparagus. It goes easily unnoticed until the brilliant flowers open in midsummer. The leaves have a hot, peppery taste and have been used to add flavour to food; beware: they can produce an unpleasant reaction in some people.

Common Rock-rose belongs to the cistus family, of which there are many species in the Mediterranean region which form large shrubs and are covered in colourful flowers – all with the same tissue-like petals, but often strongly scented. Although small, this plant's tiny stems are rather woody, a quality which it shares with its relatives. It is found only on the drier soils over chalk or limestone rock, often on slopes, or where the grass is very short. The name *Helianthemum* comes from the Greek *helios* for sun, which in this case is very apt indeed.

Grassy meadows

Biting Stonecrop *has succulent, knobbly, and tiny fleshy leaves which are lost on a stony beach until the brilliant starry flowers open to give them away.*

***Common Rock-rose's** flowers look as though they have been crafted from tissue paper, so thin and fragile are the petals on this ankle-high plant.*

Biting Stonecrop

Common Rock-rose

RANGE: Throughout Europe, except the far north of Scandinavia

RANGE: Europe, rare in Scandinavia, Ireland, Holland and Belgioum

FLOWERING TIME
A short time in June or July

FLOWERING TIME
June to September

Tormentil/Silverweed

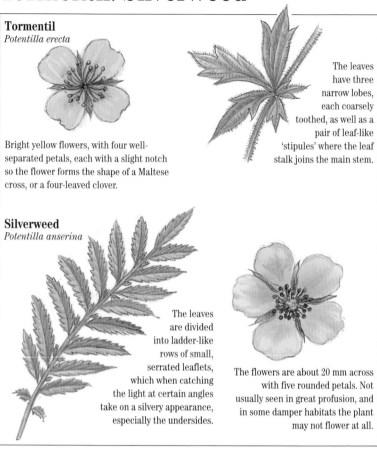

Tormentil
Potentilla erecta

Bright yellow flowers, with four well-separated petals, each with a slight notch so the flower forms the shape of a Maltese cross, or a four-leaved clover.

The leaves have three narrow lobes, each coarsely toothed, as well as a pair of leaf-like 'stipules' where the leaf stalk joins the main stem.

Silverweed
Potentilla anserina

The leaves are divided into ladder-like rows of small, serrated leaflets, which when catching the light at certain angles take on a silvery appearance, especially the undersides.

The flowers are about 20 mm across with five rounded petals. Not usually seen in great profusion, and in some damper habitats the plant may not flower at all.

Grassy meadows

Both of these species are closely related members of the rose family – typified by the numerous stamens in the centre of the flowers. **Tormentil** grows among short or tall grasses, though usually on rather acid soils. It is a weak, straggly plant, and relies on other vegetation to support it, but it has a surprisingly thick rootstock for which man has found many uses. The sap from the root is a powerful astringent used to treat diarrhoea, toothache, sore throats, warts, piles and to stem the flow of blood from cuts. It has also proved useful in tanning leather and is said to be superior to oak bark for that purpose.

The roots of **Silverweed** have also proved useful: they were dried and ground into flour, or eaten raw, but only in times of famine. The leaves were put into shoes to keep the feet cool and to prevent blisters. They are extremely soft to the touch as they are thickly covered in downy hairs, giving them their silvery appearance, though this is sometimes more easily seen at a distance than close-up. Silverweed grows on bare ground or among short grass in all sorts of situations such as wasteland or pasture, preferring moist soils, though it may also be seen on drier farm tracks.

Rough wasteland

Tormentil's small bright yellow flowers are often half-hidden in the grass. The key to identifying of these flowers is the four 'Maltese Cross' petals.

Silverweed shows as a mass of silvery leaves lying close to the ground, in certain lights, highlighted here and there by its bold flowers.

Tormentil

RANGE: Throughout Europe

FLOWERING TIME
May to September

Silverweed

RANGE: Throughout Europe,
except the extreme North

FLOWERING TIME
Sporadically from May to August

Meadow Buttercup/Lesser Spearwort

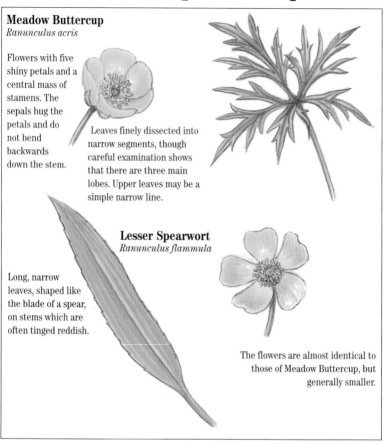

Meadow Buttercup
Ranunculus acris

Flowers with five shiny petals and a central mass of stamens. The sepals hug the petals and do not bend backwards down the stem.

Leaves finely dissected into narrow segments, though careful examination shows that there are three main lobes. Upper leaves may be a simple narrow line.

Lesser Spearwort
Ranunculus flammula

Long, narrow leaves, shaped like the blade of a spear, on stems which are often tinged reddish.

The flowers are almost identical to those of Meadow Buttercup, but generally smaller.

Grassy meadows

The sight of an early summer pasture filled with the golden flowers of **Meadow Buttercup** gladdens many people – but not farmers. In common with most members of the buttercup family, this plant is poisonous, and though grazing cattle avoid it, it grows unhindered, competing with more nutritious grass. The shiny yellow flowers have a distinctive greasy appearance, like butter, but can often be confused with other members of the family, such as Creeping Buttercup (*Ranunculus repens*) whose leaves have three broad lobes; and Bulbous Buttercup (*Ranunculus bulbosus*), one of the earliest to flower in the spring, which has sepals underneath the petals clearly bending back on themselves.

The superficially similar **Lesser Spearwort** stands apart because of its simple, spear-shaped leaves. It is restricted to moist places such as marshes or the edges of ponds, and is at its most beautiful when growing alongside the sky-blue flowers of Water Forget-me-not (page 242). The sap of buttercups is extremely acrid, and Lesser Spearwort was used to raise blisters by collecting the juice in an empty limpet shell and applying it to the skin. Its ability to inflame the skin is reflected in its specific name – *flammula*.

Ponds, ditches

Meadow Buttercup
grows to knee-height,
often abundantly,
but look at the
leaf shape to
confirm identification.

Lesser Spearwort
may also be knee-
height, but is often
shorter, and is more
likely to produce a
denser mass of flowers,
as it only grows in the
dampest places.

Meadow Buttercup

RANGE: Throughout Europe

FLOWERING TIME
Mostly in May, and sproradically until
September

Lesser Spearwort

RANGE: Throughout Europe,
except the far North

FLOWERING TIME
May to September

Lesser Celandine/Celery-leaved Buttercup

Lesser Celandine
Ranunculus ficaria

Starry yellow flowers with eight-12 pointed petals that bleach whitish as they age. The undersides are greenish, with three sepals enclosing them.

Heart-shaped, quite glossy leaves, usually a dark green and mottled with purplish markings, and sometimes burnished with bronze.

The flowers have five tiny yellow rounded petals surrounding a prominent green cone – like a miniature pineapple. The whole is 8 mm or so across.

Celery-leaved Buttercup
Ranunculus sceleratus

The leaves are lobed into three bluntly-toothed leaflets. The upper leaves are much narrower than the lower, on thick fleshy furrowed stems which resemble the stalks of an under-developed celery stick.

Woodland

The spreading golden petals of **Lesser Celandine** form a carpet of colour to reflect the sunshine of early spring. It is distinguished from other buttercups by its many petals (up to 12) and because it flowers early. However, the flowers remain steadfastly closed until morning is well advanced, revealing only the greenish underside to the petals, and even then do not open unless the sun is shining. The roots consist largely of a collection of tubers which bear some resemblance to a bunch of figs, hence the name *ficaria*. During summer and winter these tubers store the energy the plant made in spring, enabling it to burst into growth as early as February. It is normally seen in the slightly damp semi-shade of open woodland and hedgerows.

Celery-leaved Buttercup is a plant of open situations, usually with its roots in shallow water, or at least in the marginal mud of ponds or ditches; even if the soil dries out, it may continue growing in such a place for some time. Its sap is particularly acrid, and was used by street beggars to create blistered sores on their skin, and so earn extra sympathy. The sores would later be healed by applying the leaves of Mullein.

Ponds, ditches

160

Lesser Celandine *makes an ankle-deep mat of glossy leaves and flowers on woodland floors, producing the first yellow petals of spring.*

Celery-leaved Buttercup *is rather an upright plant, almost forming a miniature bush of about knee-height at the water's edge. But the tiny 'pineapples' in the flowers are the best clue.*

Lesser Celandine

RANGE: Throughout Europe, except northern Scandinavia

FLOWERING TIME
March to May

Celery-leaved Buttercup

RANGE: Throughout Europe, except the far North

FLOWERING TIME
May to September

Marsh Marigold/Yellow Water-lily

Marsh Marigold
Caltha palustris

Flowers up to 5 cm across, cup-shaped and brilliant yellow with numerous yellow stamens. The 'petals' are actually brightly coloured sepals.

Kidney-shaped, glossy green leaves with a finely toothed margin.

Dark green flask-shaped fruit that remains above the water on its stalk.

Pointed oval leaves, cleft to the middle where the stem joins; a glossy green.

Yellow Water-lily
Nuphar lutea

The flowers (about 30 mm across) are held on stalks above the water, and are globe-shaped, never opening out fully.

Marshlands

Marsh **Marigold** is actually a huge buttercup, as shown by the distinct clumps splattered with large golden flowers that it forms. It may be seen in damp, marshy grassland as well as in wet woods of birch or alder, well before the trees have burst into leaf and shrouded the woodland floor in shade. Like other marshland plants, it is declining as wetlands are drained for agriculture. The name *Caltha* comes from the Greek word for cup – describing the shape of the flowers. *Palustris* is based on a Latin word for marsh.

The leaves of **Yellow Water-lily** are the largest of any water-lily in the area covered by this guide, and may cover large expanses of water. It also produces thin translucent leaves that sit under the surface. Occasionally the plant is decimated by a species of beetle: this destroys the whole plant, so that its thick, knobbly rhizomes detach themselves from the mud and float up to the surface. The flowers attract pollinating insects by producing a strong scent of stale alcohol – coincidentally the fruit capsule recalls the shape of a brandy bottle. Yellow Water-lily may be found in all kinds of fresh water, from small ponds to large lakes or slow-moving rivers, and grows from depths of up to five metres (15 ft).

Ponds, ditches

Marsh Marigold *makes knee-high mounds of green, dotted about marshy meadows in springtime, splashed with brilliant yellow blobs of colour.*

Yellow Water-lily *is indicated by its large, slightly oval leaves on the water's surface; when the flowers are visible, the plant is unmistakeable.*

Marsh Marigold

RANGE: Throughout Europe

FLOWERING TIME
March to June

Yellow Water-lily

RANGE: Throughout Europe,
except the far North

FLOWERING TIME
June to August

Creeping Jenny

Creeping Jenny
Lysimachia nummularia

Leaves in distinct pairs on the trailing stem, each more or less rounded, and smaller towards the stem tip.

The flowers are a golden-yellow cup of five petals, but these may remain partially closed in dull weather, the petals overlapping each other. There are five large bright yellow, heart-shaped sepals beneath the flower.

Marshland

Creeping Jenny is especially delightful to find, though it can easily go unnoticed: it creeps along so close to the ground that the lush vegetation of its habitat often obscures it. It favours a variety of damp situations such as grassland, the rides and tracks of light woodland, or the marshy edges of small ponds and streams.

The name *nummularia* comes from the Latin *nummulus* meaning money, an apt description of the rounded leaves that appear in pairs along the long trailing stems, like strings of coins gradually becoming smaller and smaller along the stem's length. These leaves often become flushed with a rosy-pink hue in autumn. There is also a variety with bright yellow-green leaves that is often grown in gardens: but the leaves lack contrast to the flowers and this greatly diminishes their beauty.

Like the Scarlet Pimpernel, this is a member of the primrose family, but Creeping Jenny's petals are just joined to each other at the base, so that the flower forms a distinct cup. The flowers don't always set seed, however, but it manages to reproduce in spite of this by virtue of its long stems. These form roots at intervals, so that if a section becomes parted from its parent, it can continue growing as a new, independent plant.

Creeping Jenny's trailing stems, with its many pairs of leaves, form little ladder-patterns held tight to the ground. Both the leaves and flowers may be partially obscured by grass or other vegetation, but once discovered there is no mistaking its cup-shaped yellow flowers and twining stem.

Creeping Jenny

RANGE: Throughout most of Europe,
though avoiding northern Britain and Scandinavia

FLOWERING TIME
May to July

Wood Avens/Greater Celandine

Wood Avens
Geum urbanum

The flowers, at only 10 mm or so across, seem small for the size of the plant. They have five rounded petals and five pointed green sepals.

The fruit is a spherical mass of hooked seeds, which easily attach themselves to clothing.

The leaves are divided into three large, toothed leaflets, with two leaf-like stipules at the base of the leaf-stalk.

The flowers have four well-separated petals which are flimsy and soon fall. They go on to produce long narrow fruit capsules, (shown right).

Greater Celandine
Chelidonium majus

The leaves are divided into lobes, but with soft, rounded teeth so that each lobe resembles an oak leaf.

Woodlands

Wood Avens grows in a variety of shady situations, chiefly along woodland rides or hedgerows, but also close to human habitation – in gardens or alongside walls. This may be largely due to the tenacity with which the hooked fruits cling to clothing or dog fur, and so are easily carried home from a walk in the countryside. The three main lobes of the leaf were said to represent the Holy Trinity, and the design was much used in the decoration of medieval churches. The roots have a pleasant clove-like scent and had many medicinal uses, traditionally being dug up in the spring and dried before use.

Greater Celandine is a member of the poppy family, though the four yellow petals in the shape of a cross might lead one to believe it is related to the cabbages, such as Charlock. It occurs in similar situations to Wood Avens, though with an even greater affinity to human dwellings. The broken stems yield a thick, bright yellow sap which is very caustic and has been used to treat warts, though this is not advised as it can cause an unpleasant burn. It has a long flowering period, which is said to coincide with the presence of swallows in Europe: (the name *Chelidonium* comes from the Greek for swallow).

Rough wasteland

Wood Avens *often has luxurious knee-high leaf growth, and produces its flowers only sparsely on long stems which peep out at intervals from the undergrowth.*

Greater Celandine *occupies very similar habitats to Wood Avens. Its gently rounded leaves look and feel soft to the touch, and the flowers appear fragile.*

Wood Avens

Greater Celandine

RANGE: Throughout Europe, except the far North

FLOWERING TIME
May to September

RANGE: Throughout Europe, except northern Scandinavia and Scotland

FLOWERING TIME
May to September

167

Common Evening Primrose/Yellow Horned Poppy

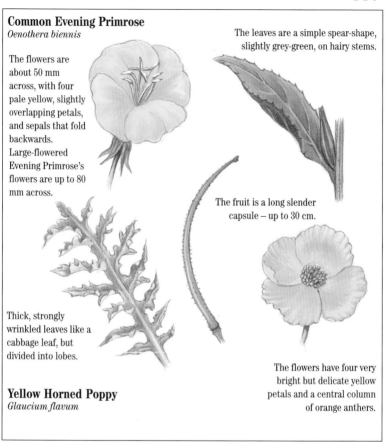

Common Evening Primrose
Oenothera biennis

The leaves are a simple spear-shape, slightly grey-green, on hairy stems.

The flowers are about 50 mm across, with four pale yellow, slightly overlapping petals, and sepals that fold backwards. Large-flowered Evening Primrose's flowers are up to 80 mm across.

The fruit is a long slender capsule – up to 30 cm.

Thick, strongly wrinkled leaves like a cabbage leaf, but divided into lobes.

Yellow Horned Poppy
Glaucium flavum

The flowers have four very bright but delicate yellow petals and a central column of orange anthers.

Rough wasteland

The pale yellow flowers of **Common Evening Primrose** do not open until the sun has almost set, but when they do, the petals unfurl with great rapidity - they open up completely from bud to moon-like disc within one or two minutes. They still look good by first thing the next morning, but by noon, or if the morning sun is strong, they shrivel and droop like wet tissue paper. The plant has been introduced from North America, and grows on disturbed sandy wasteland. It is famous for the oil extracted from the leaves which contains gamma linoleic acid – a substance that helps to balance female hormone levels. Large-flowered Evening Primrose (*Oenethera glazioviana*), which has larger flowers and red hairs on the stem, is more common in some areas of Europe such as Britain.

The **Yellow Horned Poppy** is an unmistakeable plant of shingle or sandy beaches. Like many seaside plants, it is adapted to conserving water by having thick fleshy leaves, though they retain the deeply divided shape of other poppies. Like Greater Celandine, this plant exudes a poisonous yellow latex from the cut stems. Its most extraordinary feature, however, is the long slender fruit capsule, which may be 30 cm in length.

Coast

__Common Evening Primrose's__ luminous, eerie yellow flowers, on slender stems at waist-height or more, seem to glow with their own light in the gathering dusk.

__Yellow Horned Poppy's__ bright tissue-like flowers seem incongruously delicate compared to its thick, cabbage-like leaves, growing to knee-height on shingle.

Common Evening Primrose

RANGE: Throughout Europe, though less common in the far North

FLOWERING TIME
June to September

Yellow Horned Poppy

RANGE: Southern and western coasts, northwards to south Norway

FLOWERING TIME
June to September

Primrose/Cowslip

Primrose
Primula vulgaris

The flowers all arise from the base on long stalks, but there is only one flower to a stalk, with five notched pale yellow petals and deeper yellow spots in the centre.

The leaves all arise from the base. They are oblong, tapering towards the base, and have a very wrinkled surface like old leather, and a pale mid-rib.

Cowslip
Primula veris

The leaves form a rosette close to the ground, and have a very similar surface texture to Primrose's, but they are usually much smaller and more rounded.

Flowers are in a nodding bunch of up to 30 per stalk, with a long green sepal tube, and a small tubular flower with five golden lobes opening out, each spotted with orange.

Mild weather may see **Primroses** flowering as early as December in isolated pockets, but the main showcase begins in February and March. The plant prefers slightly damp, rich soils, and though most often seen in open woodland or along hedgerows, it may turn up in surprising locations such as new motorway verges. There are two types of flower *Hedgerows, roadsides* produced, always on separate plants, whereby the anthers and stigma occupy different positions, so that cross-fertilization is assured when they are visited by long-tongued bees. Flowers of different colours can occur, typically orange, pink or brown: these may be the result of breeding with plants that have escaped from cultivation.

Cowslips prefer open, sunny situations such as dry grassland or sloping pastures on chalky soils. The flowers are only seen where there is no livestock. The leaves are loved by grazing animals, and may be included in salads, but it is the flowers which have been much prized for both medical and culinary purposes. The little yellow tubes can act as a sedative, an anti-histamine, and to reduce spasms and inflammation, but they have an even longer history as the major ingredient in Cowslip wine.

Grassy meadows

Primroses *form a natural posy of fresh green leaves and the loveliest of clean, unsullied flowers that sum up the essence of springtime.*

__Cowslip's__ nodding, dancing clusters of flowers on their own little stalks have much the same effect as primroses in pastures, but a few weeks later in the year.

Primrose

RANGE: Southern and western Europe

FLOWERING TIME
February to May, though sometimes even earlier

Cowslip

RANGE: Throughout Europe, except the far North

FLOWERING TIME
April or May

171

Autumn Hawkbit/Cat's-ear

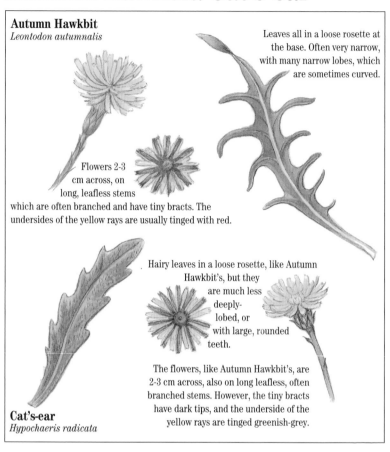

Autumn Hawkbit
Leontodon autumnalis

Leaves all in a loose rosette at the base. Often very narrow, with many narrow lobes, which are sometimes curved.

Flowers 2-3 cm across, on long, leafless stems which are often branched and have tiny bracts. The undersides of the yellow rays are usually tinged with red.

Hairy leaves in a loose rosette, like Autumn Hawkbit's, but they are much less deeply-lobed, or with large, rounded teeth.

The flowers, like Autumn Hawkbit's, are 2-3 cm across, also on long leafless, often branched stems. However, the tiny bracts have dark tips, and the underside of the yellow rays are tinged greenish-grey.

Cat's-ear
Hypochaeris radicata

Both species: grassy meadows

There are a bewildering variety of flowers that look like dandelions, all with characteristic, flat-topped yellow flowers, often consisting of ray florets and no central disc. The next few pages feature some of the most common and distinctive of these species: even so, these are generally difficult to separate without experience. Although correct identification relies on recognizing several characteristics, for each species there is often one factor which helps to point the way. The two species illustrated here are particularly tricky. **Autumn Hawkbit** may flower in midsummer, but it comes into its own as the first signs of autumn appear, and when many similar species have passed their best. Look out for the finely lobed leaves, small size and minute bracts on the leafless stems. It grows in any grassy place, though it prefers chalky soils.

Cat's-ear is very similar to Autumn Hawkbit. It, too, has leafless stems, with tiny triangular bracts all along, but the bracts do have dark-coloured tips – supposedly resembling a cat's ear. It's best to separate it by its hairy, broadly-toothed leaves and the fact that it prefers grassy situations on slightly acid soils. This in turn is best determined by finding out which other species are growing nearby. It commonly grows on lawns.

Autumn Hawkbit *looks delicate and elegant. It is rather small – not much more than ankle-height.*

Cat's-ear *is usually taller than Autumn Hawkbit, up to knee-height, and its broad-toothed hairy leaves give it a slightly coarser appearance.*

Autumn Hawkbit

RANGE: Throughout Europe

FLOWERING TIME
July to October, but mostly from August onwards

Cat's-ear

RANGE: Throughout Europe, except the far North

FLOWERING TIME
June to September

Dandelion/Colt's-foot

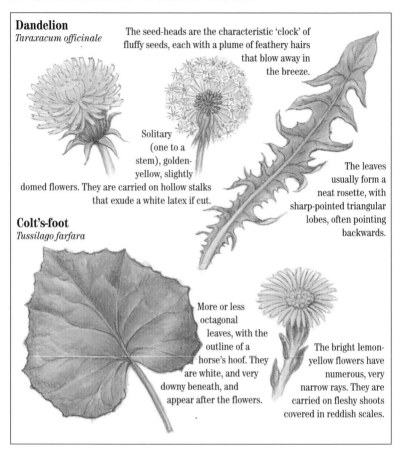

Dandelion
Taraxacum officinale

The seed-heads are the characteristic 'clock' of fluffy seeds, each with a plume of feathery hairs that blow away in the breeze.

Solitary (one to a stem), golden-yellow, slightly domed flowers. They are carried on hollow stalks that exude a white latex if cut.

The leaves usually form a neat rosette, with sharp-pointed triangular lobes, often pointing backwards.

Colt's-foot
Tussilago farfara

More or less octagonal leaves, with the outline of a horse's hoof. They are white, and very downy beneath, and appear after the flowers.

The bright lemon-yellow flowers have numerous, very narrow rays. They are carried on fleshy shoots covered in reddish scales.

The **Dandelion** is the most familiar of all the yellow daisies, and though it may be in flower at almost any time of year, there is always a spring 'flush' when whole fields and pastures, or even garden lawns, may be covered with them. Dandelions are everywhere and they owe their success partly to their long flowering-period, but also to the fact *Hedgerows, roadsides* that they set viable seed without needing to cross-fertilize with another plant. Over thousands of years, this has led to particular strains or variations remaining stable without change, and botanists recognize hundreds of 'subspecies'. The leaves may be eaten as a salad, and the roots make a poor coffee substitute.

Colt's-foot sends its peculiar shoots up very early in the spring, usually on rough, disturbed ground, and particularly on clay soils. They are thick and fleshy – rather like scaly asparagus spears. Not until the flowers have begun to set seed do the leaves appear, each with a very distinctive shape. These go on growing throughout the summer to a considerable size, storing energy in the roots to enable the shoots to flower the following spring. The leaves were a popular remedy for coughs and asthma.

Rough wasteland

Dandelion *rarely grows above ankle-height, often shorter, and creates a great show of golden, domed flower-heads in spring.*

Colt's-foot *makes very early flowers on rough ground, the stringy yellow rays sitting on top of tufts of tiny 'asparagus' spears.*

Dandelion

RANGE: Throughout Europe

FLOWERING TIME
March to October or longer, but particularly in spring

Colt's-foot

RANGE: Throughout Europe, except the extreme North

FLOWERING TIME
February to April

175

Goat's-beard/Groundsel

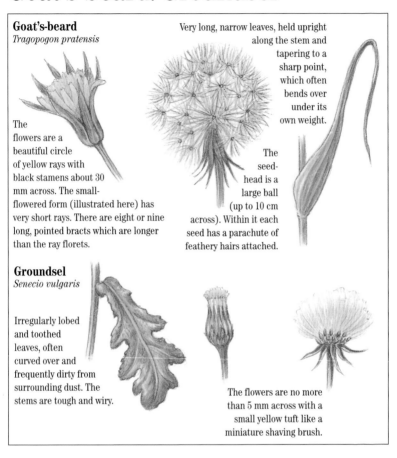

Goat's-beard
Tragopogon pratensis

Very long, narrow leaves, held upright along the stem and tapering to a sharp point, which often bends over under its own weight.

The flowers are a beautiful circle of yellow rays with black stamens about 30 mm across. The small-flowered form (illustrated here) has very short rays. There are eight or nine long, pointed bracts which are longer than the ray florets.

The seed-head is a large ball (up to 10 cm across). Within it each seed has a parachute of feathery hairs attached.

Groundsel
Senecio vulgaris

Irregularly lobed and toothed leaves, often curved over and frequently dirty from surrounding dust. The stems are tough and wiry.

The flowers are no more than 5 mm across with a small yellow tuft like a miniature shaving brush.

Grassy meadows

Somehow, **Goat's-beard** has an air of superiority: rising just above the surrounding tall grasses it looks elegant and refined. There are two forms. One, with large, dandelion-like flowers, occurs throughout most of Europe. The other has flowers that barely open, revealing a small tuft of short ray florets. In this latter form, which occurs particularly in Britain, the long pointed bracts are noticeable, forming a ring around the flower-head. In both forms the flowers close quite abruptly at about noon, whereupon the next day a new flower-bud opens. Both types go on to produce the same enormous and beautiful seed-head.

Groundsel also produces two types of flower. The commonest has stubby flower-heads that appear closed, were it not for a tuft of yellow showing at the end. Occasionally, a few short rays are produced around this disc, and then the plant takes on a new personality – more cheerful than its usual unkempt, despondent air. Like Goats-beard, this plant produces a tiny seed 'clock' of grey feathery hairs, hence its scientific name *Senecio*, from the Latin *senex* meaning old man – an allusion both to the grey hairs and to the pink receptacle left behind when they have blown away – like a tiny bald head.

Rough wasteland

Goat's-beard *is slender and regal at knee-height or more. Its flowers have a 'crown' of bracts around the petals – also present in the smaller-flowered form (see opposite). The enormous seed 'clock' is even more noticeable.*

Groundsel *is weedy, insignificant and usually not more than ankle-high. It struggles to get noticed with its barely opening flower.*

Goat's-beard	Groundsel

RANGE: Throughout Europe, except the far North	**RANGE:** Throughout Europe, except the extreme North
FLOWERING TIME July and July	**FLOWERING TIME** All year round

Common Ragwort

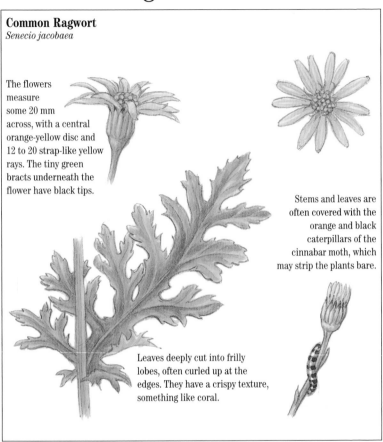

Common Ragwort
Senecio jacobaea

The flowers measure some 20 mm across, with a central orange-yellow disc and 12 to 20 strap-like yellow rays. The tiny green bracts underneath the flower have black tips.

Stems and leaves are often covered with the orange and black caterpillars of the cinnabar moth, which may strip the plants bare.

Leaves deeply cut into frilly lobes, often curled up at the edges. They have a crispy texture, something like coral.

Farmland

The sight of great swathes of Common Ragwort's yellow flowers covering fields and pastures is increasingly common to see in late summer. It loves disturbed, dry soils, so where arable fields are left fallow as set-aside, or where rabbits have dug away at embankments, this plant's frilly leaves and gold-rayed flowers soon appear. It can cause particular problems in fields heavily grazed by cattle or horses. Heavy animals pounding the soil create bare patches in the grass, where Common Ragwort's wind-born seeds alight and germinate. The plant is extremely poisonous to these animals, and they avoid it while it is fresh and green. If, however, the plant dries up or is accidentally mixed into a batch of hay, the leaves are readily eaten – resulting in hundreds of livestock deaths every year. Curiously, sheep are immune to ill effects of Common Ragwort's toxins and eat the plant with relish, so it is far less common in sheep country. The best way to control the plant is to reduce grazing pressure, meaning less soil disturbance, and to rely on the millions of cinnabar moth caterpillars who regard Ragwort as their sole foodplant. The caterpillars absorb the plant's poisons, and have bright orange and black colouring to warn birds that they too are toxic.

Common Ragwort is an untidy plant growing from knee- to waist-height. In spite of its bright colour it does little to beautify the countryside in the eyes of the farmer – see main text, opposite.

Common Ragwort

RANGE: Throughout Europe, except the far North

FLOWERING TIME
June to October

179

Fleabane/Nipplewort

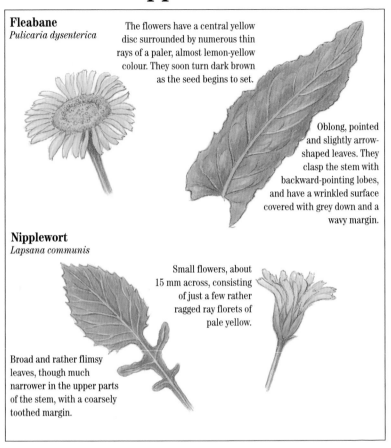

Fleabane
Pulicaria dysenterica

The flowers have a central yellow disc surrounded by numerous thin rays of a paler, almost lemon-yellow colour. They soon turn dark brown as the seed begins to set.

Oblong, pointed and slightly arrow-shaped leaves. They clasp the stem with backward-pointing lobes, and have a wrinkled surface covered with grey down and a wavy margin.

Nipplewort
Lapsana communis

Small flowers, about 15 mm across, consisting of just a few rather ragged ray florets of pale yellow.

Broad and rather flimsy leaves, though much narrower in the upper parts of the stem, with a coarsely toothed margin.

Marshland

Fleabane likes a moist soil, preferring ditches, rivers or any rough grassland where moisture is retained. If ground conditions allow, it often forms extensive colonies, spreading by creeping underground roots. The name *Pulicaria* is derived from the Latin *Pulex*, for flea. When the plant is burned, the smoke drives away fleas and other insects. Hanging bunches of it in doorways has a similar effect. The name *dysenterica* relates to its use in the past as a treatment for dysentery. When crushed, the leaves have a rather soapy smell. These woolly leaves, and the very narrow ray florets to the flowers, help distinguish it from the rest of the yellow daisy tribe.

Nipplewort is much less conspicuous. Though it relies on disturbed soils or bare ground for its seeds to take a hold, it seeks out the darker, shadier spots alongside walls, under hedgerows, and particularly in gardens. Its midsummer growth in these shady places means that it can only create a modest amount of foliage, and the stems are often lengthy and thin. This lends it a somewhat undernourished appearance. Nevertheless, its diminutive flowers shine out brightly from the gloom.

Rough wasteland

Fleabane's foliage is grey-green, almost misty in appearance, catching the eye even before the flat-topped golden flowers have appeared.

Nipplewort is much less easily noticed than Fleabane. It flowers shyly in shady corners and can grow knee-high with only a modest amount of foliage.

Fleabanet

RANGE: Mostly western and southern Europe

FLOWERING TIME
July to September

Nipplewort

RANGE: Throughout Europe, except the far North

FLOWERING TIME
May to September

Perennial Sow-thistle/Prickly Sow-thistle

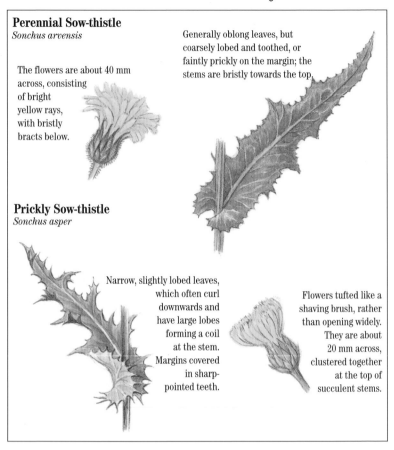

Perennial Sow-thistle
Sonchus arvensis

The flowers are about 40 mm across, consisting of bright yellow rays, with bristly bracts below.

Generally oblong leaves, but coarsely lobed and toothed, or faintly prickly on the margin; the stems are bristly towards the top.

Prickly Sow-thistle
Sonchus asper

Narrow, slightly lobed leaves, which often curl downwards and have large lobes forming a coil at the stem. Margins covered in sharp-pointed teeth.

Flowers tufted like a shaving brush, rather than opening widely. They are about 20 mm across, clustered together at the top of succulent stems.

Both species: rough wasteland

L ate summer sees the tall, hairy stems of **Perennial Sow-thistle** rising up on the margins of cultivated land, along roadsides and on wasteground. Its big yellow flower-heads look like the sun. The plant seems oblivious to the harsh, dry conditions of the late summer months, when many other plants are shrivelling up. It is similar, though bigger in every respect, to the Smooth Sow-thistle (*Sonchus oleracea*), which begins its long flowering-period much earlier in the year, and which has more deeply-lobed leaves and very pale or straw-coloured flowers.

Prickly Sow-thistle grows in similar places to (and often with) the other Sow-thistle species. It is readily identified by the curiously twirled bases of the leaves, making a shape like small ears either side of the stem. The name *Sonchus* comes from the Greek word for hollow. This is a reference to the hollow nature of the stems, which in this case are rather succulent, like celery. The stems and leaves yield a milky-white juice when broken, not dissimilar to the wild lettuce plant, and indeed the leaves of all sow-thistles may be used freely in salads. The prickles on the leaf margins of Prickly Sow-thistle make them rather unsuitable for this purpose.

Perennial Sow-thistle
*is one of the most
imposing of the yellow
daisies. It towers to
waist- or chest-height
and has the largest
flowers of the family.*

Prickly Sow-thistle
*may be just as tall and
robust as Perennial
Sow-thistle, but the
flowers are modest
and the prickly leaves
suggest a true thistle.*

Perennial Sow-thistle

RANGE: Throughout Europe,
except the extreme North

FLOWERING TIME
July to October

Prickly Sow-thistle

RANGE: Throughout Europe,
except the far North

FLOWERING TIME
June to August

Broom/Gorse

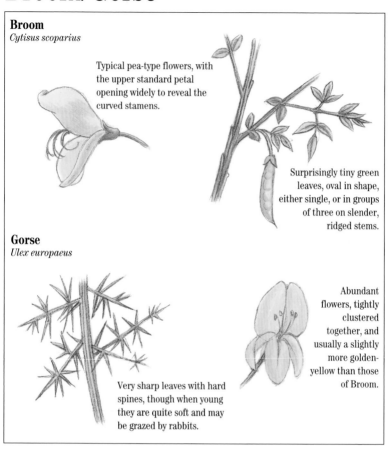

Broom
Cytisus scoparius

Typical pea-type flowers, with the upper standard petal opening widely to reveal the curved stamens.

Surprisingly tiny green leaves, oval in shape, either single, or in groups of three on slender, ridged stems.

Gorse
Ulex europaeus

Abundant flowers, tightly clustered together, and usually a slightly more golden-yellow than those of Broom.

Very sharp leaves with hard spines, though when young they are quite soft and may be grazed by rabbits.

Both species: heathland

Both of these plants are members of the pea family, and are often confused with each other at a distance, but they are different in character. **Broom** is a plant of sandy soils on heaths, coastal cliffs, woodland edges and roadsides, and has a long association with man. Its long, twiggy branches have been used for making brooms, its buds as capers, the leaves for flavouring beer, the fibre for making cloth, the bark for tanning leather, and it has many roles in medicine. Its fibrous root system helps to hold together the loose sandy banks it likes to colonize, and it has been used in road-building and to stabilize motorway embankments.

Gorse is found in similar habitats, though the two rarely grow next to each other. The dry, spiny leaves and branches are extremely flammable, which can be a serious problem on heathland in summer when very large areas may be destroyed as a result. In the past it was used on domestic fires to create sudden heat, bringing water quickly to the boil. On a warm spring day, the flowers produce a faint but delightful smell of coconut, and later in the summer, when the seed-pods are ripe, they can be heard popping open in the sun and scattering their seeds.

Broom *is elegant and somehow lady-like. Its long arching stems create a fountain-effect of colour – growing to head-height or more.*

*****Gorse*** *is rougher and tougher than Broom, growing to the same height but generating more of an explosion of colour, usually earlier in the year.*

Broom

RANGE: Throughout Europe, but avoiding much of Scandinavia

FLOWERING TIME
April to June

Gorse

RANGE: Western and southern Europe

FLOWERING TIME
January to April, but some produce flowers throughout the year

Greater Bladderwort/Common Cow-wheat

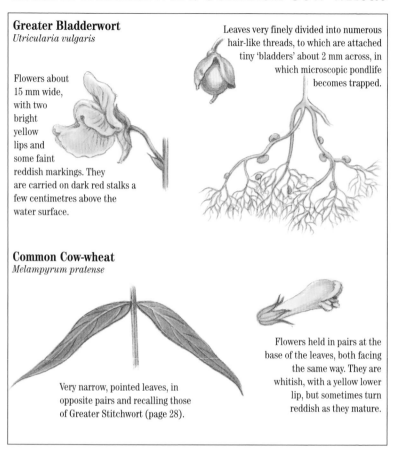

Greater Bladderwort
Utricularia vulgaris

Leaves very finely divided into numerous hair-like threads, to which are attached tiny 'bladders' about 2 mm across, in which microscopic pondlife becomes trapped.

Flowers about 15 mm wide, with two bright yellow lips and some faint reddish markings. They are carried on dark red stalks a few centimetres above the water surface.

Common Cow-wheat
Melampyrum pratense

Flowers held in pairs at the base of the leaves, both facing the same way. They are whitish, with a yellow lower lip, but sometimes turn reddish as they mature.

Very narrow, pointed leaves, in opposite pairs and recalling those of Greater Stitchwort (page 28).

Greater **Bladderwort** is not a common plant, though where it occurs it may grow in great abundance, especially where waterways have been dredged or cleaned out, giving little competition from other plants. It may go for years without producing flowers, as it

Ponds, ditches can spread vegetatively, and because it prefers very clean water which is low in nutrients. It makes up for nutrient deficiency by feeding on insects, trapping tiny pond creatures such as water-fleas in tiny sacs, which are adaptations of the leaves. There is a hair trigger on each sac, which when brushed by a passing creature causes the sac to open up suddenly, sucking the creature inside, where it is digested.

Common Cow-wheat, though belonging to a different family, is fairly closely related to Bladderwort and has the same basic pattern of two-lipped flowers. It is found on woodland rides and shady corners, and as it prefers acid soils it is at home in both coniferous or deciduous woodland. The scientific name *Melampyrum* means black wheat: the seeds of a related species of Cow-wheat (*Melampyrum arvense*) mixed in with wheat, would blacken it. Modern farming methods have made this plant extremely rare.

Woodlands

Greater Bladderwort
*is signified by
brilliant yellow
flowers on leafless
stalks dotted over the
surface of water.*

Common Cow-wheat *is an
understated plant, easily overlooked:
it lurks at ankle-height in the
undergrowth of shady woods.*

Greater Bladderwort

RANGE: Throughout Europe

FLOWERING TIME
July or August

Common Cow-wheat

RANGE: Throughout Europe

FLOWERING TIME
June to August

Black Medick/Hop Trefoil

Black Medick
Medicago lupulina

Multiple flowers in a compact head about 6 mm across. The petals wither away soon after flowering.

The leaves are 'trifoliate': they consist of three leaflets, the middle leaflet having a short stalk. The apex of each is slightly flattened, but with a small terminal tooth.

Hop Trefoil
Trifolium campestre

Flowers carried in a tight head, more oblong in shape than Black Medick's and reaching about 15 mm, remaining in place and ageing to a pale brown colour.

Trifoliate leaves, slightly more oval in shape than Black Medick's and without a terminal tooth.

Both species: rough wasteland

There are several small, clover-like, yellow-flowered members of the pea family which are hard for beginners to tell apart, and they all grow in similar situations such as cultivated fields, rough wasteland and roadsides. The medicks can be identified by their curious miniature seed-pods, which curl up into different shapes according to the species. In **Black Medick** they form a coil which ripens to black, several of them clumped together into an oblong, knobbly head. Spotted Medick (*Medicago arabica*) has small spiny pods which coil up like a snail shell, with a hole through the middle, and there is a black spot on each leaflet. Lesser Trefoil (*Trifolium dubium*) has very similar leaves and flowers, but the ripening pod remains in the shelter of the sepals and cannot be seen.

Hop Trefoil has pods which do the same, but as the sepals age, they inflate slightly and turn pale brown, so that the flower-head resembles a miniature hop. All of these clover-type plants are very palatable to grazing animals as well as insects, and as the season progresses the leaves are often nibbled away at the edges. Their advantage as a fodder crop is increased by the fact that bacteria in their roots helps to return nourishing nitrates to the soil.

Black Medick
sprawls untidily through rough grassland at ankle-height or just over: it is difficult to tell where one plant stops and another begins.

Hop Trefoil has a slightly neater, bushier appearance than Black Medick, usually carrying an abundance of brown, hop-like fruits.

Black Medick

RANGE: Throughout Europe, except the far North

FLOWERING TIME
May to August

Hop Trefoil

RANGE: Throughout Europe, except the far North

FLOWERING TIME
June to September

Common Bird's-foot Trefoil

Common Bird's-foot Trefoil
Ornithopus perpusillus

Flowers are in ring-like cluster, each the typical pea-shape with a red-streaked upper lip.

Fruits are long and ripen to dark brown, with a claw-like hair at the tip, so that the cluster resembles a bird's foot.

Leaves appear to be three-lobed, but have an extra pair of leaflets at the base of the stalk.

Grassy meadows

Bird's-foot Trefoil often occurs in great abundance, producing masses of egg-yolk yellow flowers, sometimes streaked with orange or entirely orange, and with vermilion flower-buds. The true wild form tends to keep very low to the ground, forming a golden carpet of flowers. A variety of the wild form produces taller, bushier plants and may be seen as a fodder crop. The plant is very palatable to grazing animals and is a perennial, continuing to grow and self-sow for a long period. Although it is relatively slow-growing, it can withstand much drier, warmer conditions than many of its clover-type relatives. In common with other members of the pea family, bacteria in its special root-nodules can fix nitrogen in the soil, acting as a natural fertilizer or 'green manure'. Bird's-foot Trefoil is poisonous to humans. It has received attention recently as a possible treatment for cancer, and for reducing muscle spasms. The flowers have sedative properties, and perhaps not surprisingly, yield an orange-yellow dye.

Greater Bird's-foot Trefoil (*Lotus uliginosus*) is a similar plant to Bird's-foot Trefoil, though always taller and with flowers always remaining yellow. It prefers damp marshy sites, and usually grows among taller vegetation.

Common Bird's-foot Trefoil forms mounds suffused with yellow at anything from ankle- to knee-height, making it always a pleasure to see. A diminutive member of the pea family, with a prostrate habit, this plant is worth looking at close up.

Common Bird's-foot Trefoil

RANGE: Throughout Europe,
except the extreme North

FLOWERING TIME
Continuously flowers from May through to September

Kidney Vetch/Meadow Vetchling

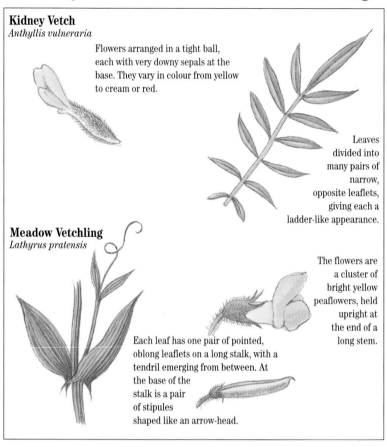

Kidney Vetch
Anthyllis vulneraria

Flowers arranged in a tight ball, each with very downy sepals at the base. They vary in colour from yellow to cream or red.

Leaves divided into many pairs of narrow, opposite leaflets, giving each a ladder-like appearance.

Meadow Vetchling
Lathyrus pratensis

The flowers are a cluster of bright yellow peaflowers, held upright at the end of a long stem.

Each leaf has one pair of pointed, oblong leaflets on a long stalk, with a tendril emerging from between. At the base of the stalk is a pair of stipules shaped like an arrow-head.

Both species: grassy meadows

It is hard to pinpoint the colour of **Kidney Vetch** flowers. They are usually bright yellow, but they may also be cream, orange or red, and as the individual flowers fade they become a rusty brown. Their most notable feature, however, is the woolly base to each flower, caused by thick downy hairs on the sepals, which gives the whole flower-head a cottony appearance. It occurs in short grassland on chalky soils, particularly near the sea, typically on cliffs, but it may be equally at home on road embankments and motorway verges or on sand dunes. It was used as an ancient remedy for wounds and skin eruptions, perhaps due to the absorbent nature of its woolly flower-heads.

Like other *Lathyrus* species, **Meadow Vetchling** is a climbing plant, but in this case it limits its athleticism to twining around the stems of grasses in open, sunny meadows, on a variety of soils. The long, curling tendrils which the plant uses to support itself are actually extensions of the leaf rather than the stem, and the pair of oval 'leaves' at the base of the tendril are simply leaflets. The plant may be readily recognized, however, even when it is not in flower by the distinctly arrow-shaped 'stipules' – modified leaves which occur at the base of the leaf-stalk.

__Kidney Vetch__ is a low, tufted plant, usually at ankle-height, whose white downy blobs of flowers look characteristic, even at a distance.

__Meadow Vetchling__ is more inclined than Kidney Vetch to be half-hidden among long grasses, with its tight clusters of flowers peeping through in a scattered fashion.

Kidney Vetch	*Meadow Vetchling*

RANGE: Throughout Europe, except the extreme North	**RANGE:** Throughout Europe, except most of Iceland
FLOWERING TIME June to September	**FLOWERING TIME** May to August

Sun Spurge/Cypress Spurge

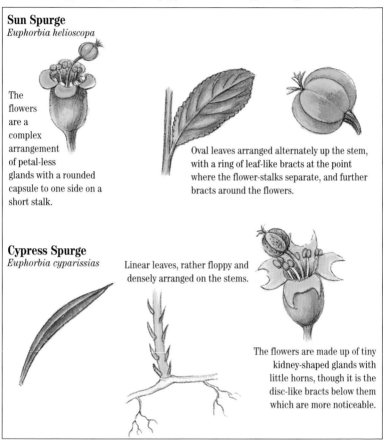

Sun Spurge
Euphorbia helioscopa

The flowers are a complex arrangement of petal-less glands with a rounded capsule to one side on a short stalk.

Oval leaves arranged alternately up the stem, with a ring of leaf-like bracts at the point where the flower-stalks separate, and further bracts around the flowers.

Cypress Spurge
Euphorbia cyparissias

Linear leaves, rather floppy and densely arranged on the stems.

The flowers are made up of tiny kidney-shaped glands with little horns, though it is the disc-like bracts below them which are more noticeable.

Farmland

Sun Spurge produces flowers in a circle of smaller circles, facing directly upwards and mirroring the sun with an almost unnatural yellow-green colour. It is commonly seen at the margins of fields or among arable crops, wherever the soil has been cultivated. Rabbits and deer keep well away from it: in common with other spurges, the plant exudes a thick, milky sap which is toxic if eaten, and intensely irritating to the skin, causing photo-sensitization – a severe rash develops when the skin is exposed to sunlight. As a result, the juice has been used to treat warts, though it is extremely inadvisable to do so. The sap is thought to be a potential source of latex, for making rubber.

Cypress Spurge is a rather attractive plant, whose hundreds of narrow leaves arranged around the stems give it the appearance of a young fir tree. It grows in a variety of habitats, though usually on chalky soils with only a sparse covering of vegetation, such as abandoned fields, roadsides, open woods and rocky sites. A spray of bright yellow flowers is produced, which gradually take on a reddish hue, becoming entirely red by midsummer: in fact, the colour is in the disc-like bracts below the true flowers.

Grassy meadows

194

Sun Spurge *appears as a collection of acid-yellow discs between ankle- and knee-height, easily spotted either among other vegetation or on bare soil.*

Cypress Spurge *is a much bushier plant than Sun Spurge, though the same height. It looks like a miniature conifer tree until the multi-coloured flowers appear.*

Sun Spurge

RANGE: Throughout Europe, except the far North

FLOWERING TIME
May to August

Cypress Spurge

RANGE: Europe except northern Britain and Scandinavia

FLOWERING TIME
April to July

Yellow Archangel/Common Toadflax

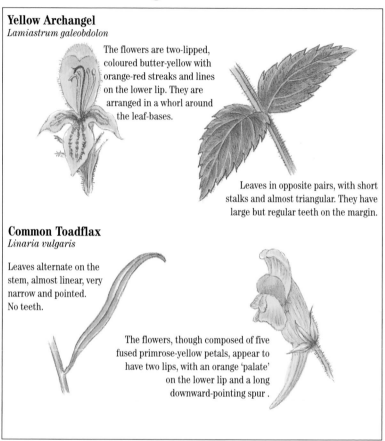

Yellow Archangel
Lamiastrum galeobdolon

The flowers are two-lipped, coloured butter-yellow with orange-red streaks and lines on the lower lip. They are arranged in a whorl around the leaf-bases.

Leaves in opposite pairs, with short stalks and almost triangular. They have large but regular teeth on the margin.

Common Toadflax
Linaria vulgaris

Leaves alternate on the stem, almost linear, very narrow and pointed. No teeth.

The flowers, though composed of five fused primrose-yellow petals, appear to have two lips, with an orange 'palate' on the lower lip and a long downward-pointing spur .

Woodlands

Woodland rides and margins, shady hedgerows and coppices are the favoured habitats of **Yellow Archangel**, generally on heavier, clay soils. It bears a close resemblance to its relative, the White Dead-nettle, but is much more local in its appearance. It was an effective treatment for healing sores and ulcers, and the young flowering shoots may be boiled and eaten – but some think it too pretty to be used for that purpose. There is a garden variety which frequently escapes into the wild, spreading to form fairly extensive colonies by means of creeping roots. It has silver and green mottled leaves, and like many garden cultivars, the 'lily has been gilded too much' and the wild form is far more attractive.

Common Toadflax is found on roadsides; field edges; along hedges bordering meadows and on dry grassy banks, but usually where there is a little shelter. The mouth of the flower is kept tight shut by the pressure of the two 'lips' that form it, giving it, some say, the expression of a toad. The mouth can only be opened by large insects such as bumble bees, which also possess the long tongue needed to reach the nectar at the base of the long spur. By this means it ensures effective pollen transfer from one flower to another.

Hedgerows, roadsides

Yellow Archangel is one of those spring flowers that lifts the heart: it is always neatly turned out, and gives you a sense of a happy discovery.

Common Toadflax flowers have a pale, greenish-yellow hue that makes them recognizable on the roadside even when speeding past.

Yellow Archangel

Common Toadflax

RANGE: Most of Europe, but avoiding northern Britain and most of Scandinavia

FLOWERING TIME
For a short period between April and June

RANGE: Throughout Europe, except the extreme North

FLOWERING TIME
July to October

197

Crosswort/Bog Asphodel

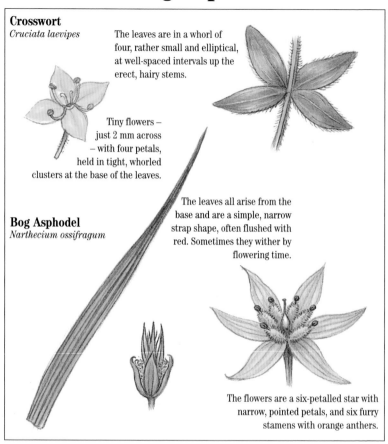

Crosswort
Cruciata laevipes

The leaves are in a whorl of four, rather small and elliptical, at well-spaced intervals up the erect, hairy stems.

Tiny flowers – just 2 mm across – with four petals, held in tight, whorled clusters at the base of the leaves.

Bog Asphodel
Narthecium ossifragum

The leaves all arise from the base and are a simple, narrow strap shape, often flushed with red. Sometimes they wither by flowering time.

The flowers are a six-petalled star with narrow, pointed petals, and six furry stamens with orange anthers.

The tiny four-petalled flowers of **Crosswort** show that it is a member of the bedstraw family, but rather than the usual spreading, fluffy habit of those plants, this one has erect stems with its flowers tucked in close to each whorl of leaves (which form a cross). Like some other *Hedgerows, roadsides* members of the family, a red dye can be got from the roots and was used for dressing wounds. The entire plant has an unusual yellowish-green colour, as though it were sickly or lacking light, which helps one to pick it out easily among the tall grasses of roadsides, hedgebanks, scrubby-places and the margins of pastures. It usually grows close to some taller, sheltering vegetation, because it cannot withstand the full heat of the sun.

Bog Asphodel is a charming plant, worth seeking out, but be prepared to step through saturated floating mats of vegetation in a bog in order make the discovery. It is restricted to the highly acidic soils of bogs, moors and heaths, often on hills and mountains. Within the star of yellow petals there are six stamens, whose filaments are covered with fine yellow hairs, like a microscopic bottle-brush. The flowers produce brilliant orange fruit-capsules, so that colonies of the plant look like flames scattered over the heath.

Heathland

198

Crosswort's *individual flowers are not especially noticeable. What you see instead are the almost misty, yellow-green knee-high patches it forms alongside hedgerows.*

Bog Asphodel's *brilliant yellow flowers draw the eye, often forming large colonies at ankle-height.*

Crosswort

RANGE: Central and southern Europe, avoiding Scandinavia and Ireland

FLOWERING TIME
April to June

Bog Asphodel

RANGE: Britain and Ireland, western Scandinavia, Denmark

FLOWERING TIME
July to September

Yellow-rattle

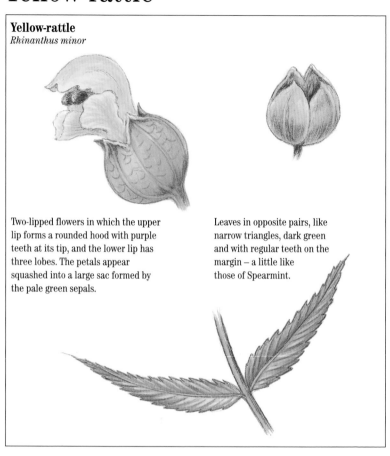

Yellow-rattle
Rhinanthus minor

Two-lipped flowers in which the upper lip forms a rounded hood with purple teeth at its tip, and the lower lip has three lobes. The petals appear squashed into a large sac formed by the pale green sepals.

Leaves in opposite pairs, like narrow triangles, dark green and with regular teeth on the margin – a little like those of Spearmint.

Grassy meadows

Yellow-rattle has an unusual quality which it shares with some other members of its family, such as Eyebright (page 44) and Red Bartsia (page 120). It is an annual, growing fresh from seed each year, and yet it can establish itself in densely-packed grasslands that are full of competing perennials. Normally, annuals cannot stand this sort of competition, preferring bare ground where they can quickly establish large root systems unhindered. Yellow-rattle overcomes this by being partially parasitic on grasses: its germinating seed gets water and nutrients from the roots of neighbouring plants instead of generating a large root network of its own. As a side-effect, grass growth is held somewhat in check, and other herbaceous plants encouraged. This often results in a very flower-rich grassland. An obvious feature of the curiously-shaped flowers is the large green sepals that surround the base of the petals. These form a narrow tube inside the protective envelope of the sepals, as though they were in the centre of a balloon. This stops insects from biting through the sepals to steal the nectar from the base of the petal tube; instead they have to enter by the conventional route and pollinate the plant. These sepals inflate further when the seed is formed, which can be heard rattling inside when the plant has dried out.

Yellow-rattle can be seen as troops of upright stems with ranks of one-sided yellow flowers half-hidden in the long grass, from which it derives the water and minerals that it needs to survive. When ripe and dry its seeds rattle when moved by the wind.

Yellow-rattle

RANGE: Throughout Europe

FLOWERING TIME
Between May and August

Wild Mignonette/Weld

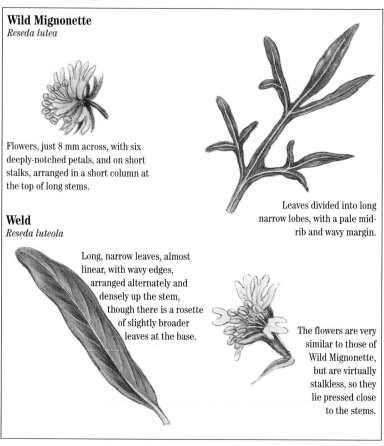

Wild Mignonette
Reseda lutea

Flowers, just 8 mm across, with six deeply-notched petals, and on short stalks, arranged in a short column at the top of long stems.

Leaves divided into long narrow lobes, with a pale mid-rib and wavy margin.

Weld
Reseda luteola

Long, narrow leaves, almost linear, with wavy edges, arranged alternately and densely up the stem, though there is a rosette of slightly broader leaves at the base.

The flowers are very similar to those of Wild Mignonette, but are virtually stalkless, so they lie pressed close to the stems.

Grassy meadows

These two plants are almost different versions of the same thing, indeed the Latin names are very similar: *lutea* means yellow, and *luteola* means yellowish. They may even be found growing together, preferring disturbed soils in dry stony places, field margins, old quarries, wasteland or bare grassland, but always preferring chalky soils.

The petals of the **Wild Mignonette** flower are rather complex. There are six of them, and the upper, middle and lower petals have different shapes, forked into narrow lobes so that the flower as a whole has a fluffy look, an appearance which is accentuated when the flowers are seen *en masse*. The fruits of the plant are shaped rather like a cylindrical pot or amphora: they open at the top, and are ranked along the stems in increasing numbers as the flowers continue to develop above.

Weld has narrower leaves and flower spikes than Wild Mignonette, and appears in considerable quantity to form a miniature forest where the plant has taken hold. The plant is biennial, so in its first year there is little more to be seen than a tight rosette of leaves close to the ground. It was planted for its yellow dye, now superceded by chemical products.

Rough wasteland

Wild Mignonette *forms a large tuft, knee-high or more, topped with fluffy candles of creamy-yellow flowers.*

__Weld__ is similar to Wild Mignonette in many ways, but its habit is different, with long thin spikes of flowers towering to head-height – though it may be much shorter.

Wild Mignonette

RANGE: Throughout Europe, except the far North

FLOWERING TIME
May to September

Weld

RANGE: Similar distribution, though it reaches further South

FLOWERING TIME
June to September

Ribbed Melilot/Agrimony

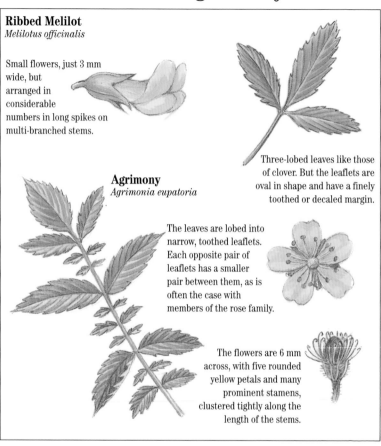

Ribbed Melilot
Melilotus officinalis

Small flowers, just 3 mm wide, but arranged in considerable numbers in long spikes on multi-branched stems.

Three-lobed leaves like those of clover. But the leaflets are oval in shape and have a finely toothed or decaled margin.

Agrimony
Agrimonia eupatoria

The leaves are lobed into narrow, toothed leaflets. Each opposite pair of leaflets has a smaller pair between them, as is often the case with members of the rose family.

The flowers are 6 mm across, with five rounded yellow petals and many prominent stamens, clustered tightly along the length of the stems.

Rough wasteland

Ribbed Melilot is native to southern Europe, but has been introduced further north: it is yet another member of the pea family which has been used as a fodder crop. At one time, particularly in the 16th century, it was cultivated extensively for that purpose, but became superceded by Red Clover and Sainfoin, and latterly by chemical fertilizers. The scientific name *Melilotus* comes from *Mel* meaning honey – a reference to the great attraction that the plant has for bees. It smells of new mown hay because the leaves contain coumarin: a property which made it useful as a packing material for linen and for fur coats as it deters moths. Because of the sweet scent, it was also used as a flavouring for snuff and tobacco.

Walking through a stand of **Agrimony**, especially with a dog, is to be avoided: the hooked fruits which line the stems cling on to fur or fabric with remarkable tenacity. In spite of this disadvantage, the plant has proved very useful, for the leaves make an agreeable drink if added to China tea, giving it a distinctive flavour. Agrimony was also used to treat wounds, and modern research indicates that it has anti-viral properties.

Grassy meadows

204

Ribbed Melilot *forms a waist- to chest-high, untidy scramble of ascending yellow spires along roadsides.*

Agrimony *is much neater than Ribbed Melilot, sending up regular vertical spires to waist-height above the surrounding grassland.*

Ribbed Melilot

RANGE: Throughout Europe, except the far North

FLOWERING TIME
July to September

Agrimony

RANGE: Throughout Europe, except the extreme North

FLOWERING TIME
June to August

Dark Mullein/Great Mullein

Dark Mullein
Verbascum nigrum

The flowers have five rounded yellow petals, and five prominent, furry purple stamens, with orange anthers.

Dark, glossy green oblong leaves with a red mid-rib, a short stalk and a neatly toothed margin.

Great Mullein
Verbascum thapsus

Each flower has five broad, rounded yellow petals, with white hairs on the stamens. The flowers never open all at once but at more or less irregular intervals along the stem.

Large leaves with no stalks. Densely packed, with an untoothed margin, and a soft texture, like felt.

The flowers of **Dark Mullein** have the most extraordinary stamens: their filaments are covered with fine hairs, so they look like a bottle-brush. Moreover, they are purple, which seems incongruous against the yellow background of the petals. The female stigma matures well before *Hedgerows, roadsides* the stamens, which ensures that self-pollination cannot occur at this stage and that any visiting insect is likely to bring pollen from a different flower – a strategy known as protogyny. As an insurance, the stamens will brush pollen from their anthers on to the stigma at a later stage: making self-fertilization better than none at all.

Great Mullein is distinguished by its velvety leaves, even in its first year when they appear as a felted rosette without any flowering spike. The thick downy hairs which cover the leaves serve many functions. They act as a preventative against insects who find it impossible to get through to the succulent flesh of the leaf, and they are also an irritant to the mucous membranes of grazing animals. They help to conserve moisture by making a humid atmosphere near the leaf surface, although the damp atmosphere can encourage mould growth. They are flammable when dry and have been pressed into lamp wicks.

Rough wasteland

206

Dark Mullein *appears as slender but sturdy, vertical knee- to waist-height columns, densely covered with yellow flowers.*

Great Mullein *usually reaches head-height, with obvious felt-textured leaves at the base and a tall spire intermittently dotted with yellow flowers.*

Dark Mullein

Great Mullein

RANGE: Throughout Europe, avoiding the far North and western Britain

RANGE: Throughout Europe, except the far North

FLOWERING TIME
June to September

FLOWERING TIME
June to August

207

Yellow Loosestrife

Yellow Loosestrife
Lysimachia vulgaris

The flowers have five oval, bright yellow petals, sometimes slightly orange in the centre. They go on to produce spherical fruit capsules (shown below).

Pointed oval leaves, in whorls of four lower down the stem, in whorls of three higher up, and in opposite pairs at the top.

Marshland

The name *Lysimachia* appears to be derived from that of Lysimachus, a general under Alexander the Great in about 300 BC and later King of Thrace. He reputedly discovered the healing virtues of this plant: the leaves, applied to a fresh wound, were said to stem bleeding in a short time. However, the word also comes from the Greek for 'release from worry', and it is said that the plant is an effective deterrent against biting insects: tied around the necks of nervous cattle it can calm them if bothered by flies. Some accounts even merge these two explanations. Whatever its role in the past, it does have some medicinal properties (as an astringent), and may also be used to treat stomach disorders. Yellow Loosestrife will only grow where the soil is permanently damp, and in spite of its tall stature it is not very robust. Easily blown over, it usually occurs among other tall vegetation in marshes, fens, wet meadows and streamsides.

Dotted Loosestrife (*Lysimachia punctata*) is a plant from southeastern Europe which is widely grown in gardens and has now become naturalized throughout Europe. It favours drier soils than Yellow Loosestrife and has a much neater arrangement of flowers in tall columns, each with an orange blotch at the centre.

Yellow Loosestrife grows up to chest-height, and pushes its bold, compact pyramids of flowers up above the tall surrounding vegetation in marshes and fens. It used to be burned in houses to clear the rooms of flies and gnats and it also had many other uses (see main text).

Yellow Loosestrife

RANGE: Throughout Europe,
except the far North

FLOWERING TIME
July and August

Winter-cress/Charlock

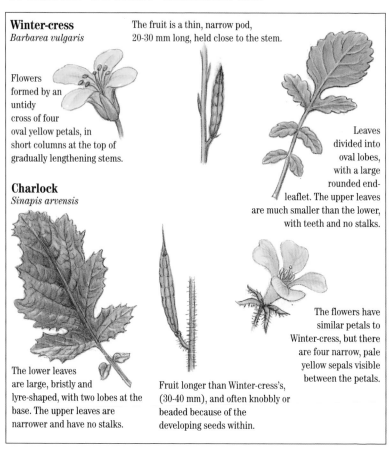

Winter-cress
Barbarea vulgaris

The fruit is a thin, narrow pod, 20-30 mm long, held close to the stem.

Flowers formed by an untidy cross of four oval yellow petals, in short columns at the top of gradually lengthening stems.

Charlock
Sinapis arvensis

Leaves divided into oval lobes, with a large rounded end-leaflet. The upper leaves are much smaller than the lower, with teeth and no stalks.

The flowers have similar petals to Winter-cress, but there are four narrow, pale yellow sepals visible between the petals.

The lower leaves are large, bristly and lyre-shaped, with two lobes at the base. The upper leaves are narrower and have no stalks.

Fruit longer than Winter-cress's, (30-40 mm), and often knobbly or beaded because of the developing seeds within.

Ponds, ditches

There are many yellow-flowered members of the cabbage family, including Wild Cabbage (*Brassica oleracea*) itself, which is a rather rare plant of coastal cliffs. They all have the characteristic flower-shape of four oval petals forming a cross, and can be extremely difficult to differentiate. Winter-cress and Charlock are two of the most common.

Winter-cress likes disturbed soil, but only in damp situations, so it may turn up next to roadside drainage ditches as well as by ponds and streams. The lower leaves are held in great esteem as a salad vegetable that can be picked in the winter, provided the plant is encouraged by regular harvesting of the leaves and the flowers are not allowed to set seed.

Charlock is a weed of arable fields. It used to be a serious pest, but modern farming herbicides have eradicated it from most fields. It is still common, however, on field margins, wasteground or among organic crops. The seeds make a useful substitute for mustard seeds; the leaves are edible, but rather coarse. Rape (*Brassica napus*) has a similar appearance, but it is a good deal taller. It is very widely planted for its oil – producing seeds and frequently escapes from farms to the wider countryside.

Farmland

Winter-cress sends up open columns of flowers in candelabra fashion, generally at about knee-height, though sometimes taller.

Charlock is a looser, less tidy plant than Winter-cress, with a jumble of flower clusters spreading in all directions, and usually a little taller.

Winter-cress

RANGE: Throughout Europe

FLOWERING TIME
Mostly in May or June, but may
continue into August

Charlock

RANGE: Throughout Europe

FLOWERING TIME
May to October

211

Wallflower/Hedge Mustard

Wallflower
Erysimum cheiri

The fruit is a long, slender pod up to 75 mm long.

The flowers have four broad petals coloured yellow, or (frequently) orange-brown. Garden varieties that have escaped may be white, pink or mauve.

Long and narrow leaves. They are rough and hairy, densely arranged on tough woody stems.

Tiny flowers, just 3 mm across, clustered tightly at the tip of the stem. Below them, the narrow fruits are pressed close to the stems.

Hedge Mustard
Sisymbrium officinale

Leaves divided into jagged, toothed lobes, the points turning back towards the stem.

Rough wasteland

The **Wallflower** is native to southern Greece, but as a result of its natural beauty and endearing growth habit, has been introduced since medieval times to every part of Europe warm enough to sustain it. Its natural habitat is the smallest of ledges on cliffs, but is more frequently found on old stonework and ruins of castles and city walls. Doubtless it has been deliberately sown in such sites to add to their decaying picturesque, but it is perfectly able to grow wherever it pleases. A delightful scent adds to its appeal, extracted as an oil and used as perfume.

Hedge Mustard is at the opposite end of the scale in terms of attraction from the Wallflower. It is a weed of bare ground, waste-places and the margins of arable fields, which likes to germinate in recently disturbed soil, and so often associates with poppies. Its preference for such locations, and a slight roughness to the leaves, mean that it is invariably covered in dust, though the leaves are edible. The plant was not always considered without value however: Louis XIV thought it an excellent remedy for loss of voice, and it has been known as the 'singer's plant'.

Farmland

Wallflower *forms a colourful bush-like splash of orange-yellow on old walls and cliffs.*

Hedge Mustard *is a rather insignificant, unattractive plant, with a wiry candelabra of slender, curving stems.*

Wallflower

Hedge Mustard

RANGE: Introduced to western and southern Europe

RANGE: Throughout Europe, except the far North

FLOWERING TIME
April to June

FLOWERING TIME
Continuously from May to September

213

Goldenrod/Perforate St John's-wort

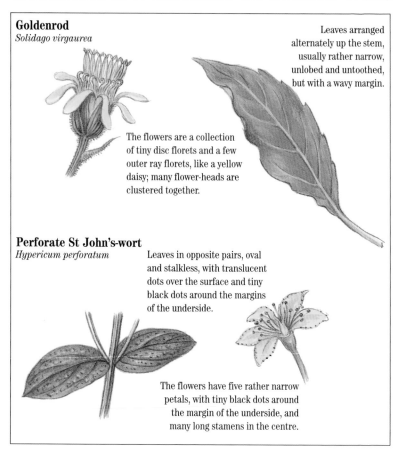

Goldenrod
Solidago virgaurea

Leaves arranged alternately up the stem, usually rather narrow, unlobed and untoothed, but with a wavy margin.

The flowers are a collection of tiny disc florets and a few outer ray florets, like a yellow daisy; many flower-heads are clustered together.

Perforate St John's-wort
Hypericum perforatum

Leaves in opposite pairs, oval and stalkless, with translucent dots over the surface and tiny black dots around the margins of the underside.

The flowers have five rather narrow petals, with tiny black dots around the margin of the underside, and many long stamens in the centre.

It is difficult to pin down **Golden Rod's** preferred habitat: it can occur in open woods, along roadsides, among rocks or in grassy places. Although it always likes dry soil, it is often absent in apparently suitable places. The leaves and flowers produce a yellow dye, and the whole plant *Hedgerows, roadsides* contains tannin. It was considered excellent as a diuretic and for treating kidney disorders. Canadian Goldenrod (*Solidago canadensis*) was introduced to Europe as a garden plant: it grows much taller than Goldenrod, with one-sided tiers of flowers, and has also established itself in the wild, forming huge colonies on wasteground.

There are several species of St John's-wort, many of which look terribly similar, but **Perforate St John's-wort** is one of the most common and may be identified by its round stems with minute 'wings' running along their length. Its leaves are also diagnostic: hold one up to the light and you will see it peppered with tiny, translucent dots. These dots contain an oil which shows considerable medical promise as an anti-depressant, also for bladder and lung complaints. The plant has a strong smell, which supposedly warded off evil spirits, and it was hung over religious paintings to protect them.

Grassy meadows

Goldenrod *always manages to look pretty although somewhat untidy, with its upright stems bearing a jumble of golden-yellow flowers at knee-height.*

Perforate St John's-wort *is also knee-high, and has a slightly more spreading habit and a somewhat delicate look. Its flowers are gathered at the top.*

Goldenrod

RANGE: Throughout Europe, except Iceland

FLOWERING TIME
July to September

Perforate St John's-wort

RANGE: Throughout Europe, except the far North

FLOWERING TIME
May to September

Lady's Bedstraw/Common Meadow Rue

Lady's Bedstraw
Galium verum

The leaves are whorls of eight to 12 tiny, linear leaflets arranged around the thin, wiry stems. They are easily recognized, often creeping along the ground.

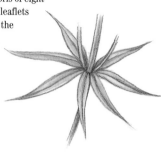

The flowers have four tiny petals and are just 2 mm across, but are produced in a foaming mass.

Common Meadow Rue
Thalictrum flavum

The leaves are divided into characteristically-shaped lobes, usually with three pointed teeth, though sometimes they may be rounded.

The flowers are simply a mass of long, white drooping filaments with yellow anthers, sometimes with four creamy sepals at the base, which soon fall off.

Grassy meadows

Lady's Bedstraw is a delightful plant to come across on dry, grassy banks, roadsides, hillsides and cliff-top lawns. It is attractive to look at, and it has an equally attractive smell (when dried) of new-mown hay due to the presence of coumarin in the leaves. As a stuffing for mattresses, it kept fleas and bed-bugs at bay. The plant has numerous applications: for kidney disorders; as a treatment for epilepsy; for reducing inflammation and healing wounds. It was used as a vegetable rennet in cheese-making, (*Galium* comes from the Greek for milk) imparting a rich yellow colour to the cheese (it also yields a yellow dye). Recent attempts to use these qualities commercially have met with little success.

Common Meadow Rue is one of the members of the buttercup family that looks nothing like a buttercup. The reproductive parts of a flower determine which family it belongs to. Meadow rue has the same rounded cluster of female ovaries and numerous long stamens as all buttercups. It has no petals: instead pollinating insects are attracted to the long drooping filaments of the stamens with their yellow anthers. It is found in wet grassy habitats, fens and marshes, among tall vegetation, preferring chalky soils.

Marshland

216

Lady's Bedstraw *produces a fluffy mass of flowers like greenish-yellow candyfloss. It grows up to knee-height, but sometimes it is shorter.*

Common Meadow Rue is waist- to- chest-height, supporting a foam of creamy-yellow flowers above surrounding vegetation.

Lady's Bedstraw

RANGE: Throughout Europe, except the extreme North

FLOWERING TIME
June to September

Common Meadow Rue

RANGE: Throughout Europe, except northern and western Britain

FLOWERING TIME
July to August

217

Wild Parsnip/Tansy

Wild Parsnip
Pastinaca sativa

The flowers are a flat-topped umbel, 4-10 cm across, of tiny yellow florets, themselves arranged in smaller umbels.

Leaves divided into flat, coarsely toothed lobes. The lower leaves have stalks while the upper leaves are stalkless.

Tansy
Tanacetum vulgare

Leaves divided into many opposite, narrow lobes which are sharply toothed, like the frond of a fern.

The flowers are a dense collection of disc florets, forming a tight rounded 'button' with a flat top. Several of the 'buttons' are concentrated together in a cluster.

Grassy meadows

There are a few yellow-flowered members of the carrot family, but **Wild Parsnip** is distinctive, forming extensive colonies alongside roads, on embankments or in rough grassland, preferring chalky soils. It is the plant from which the cultivated vegetable was derived, providing a frost-resistant root throughout the winter with excellent food value. The leaves and young shoots may also be eaten if cooked. The sap contains a chemical, xanthotoxin, which causes photosensitivity: so if you walk through a stand of Wild Parsnip with bare legs, a severe rash may develop when the skin is exposed to sunlight.

Tansy is a tall, attractive herb easily identified by its clusters of golden buttons, though the fern-like leaves are also characteristic. It has a history of use as a strewing herb – spread about the house to repel insects. When grown with fruit trees it can also keep away pests, though it is attractive to pollinating insects such as hoverflies. Tansy has also been drunk as a tea to expel intestinal worms, but the leaves do contain a toxin and such use is considered extremely dangerous. The plant thrives on a variety of soils, but is most often seen on roadsides, on disturbed wasteground, or cultivated fields.

Hedgerows, roadsides

Wild Parsnip makes flat-topped platforms of yellow flowers at about waist-height in late summer, rather like a yellow form of Hogweed.

Tansy grows to the same height as Wild Pansy, or taller, but with flat tops of golden coins above a mass of fern-like leaves.

Wild Parsnip

Tansy

RANGE: Throughout Europe, except northern Scandinavia and northern Britain

FLOWERING TIME
July and August

RANGE: Throughout Europe

FLOWERING TIME
July to September

219

Lords-and-Ladies

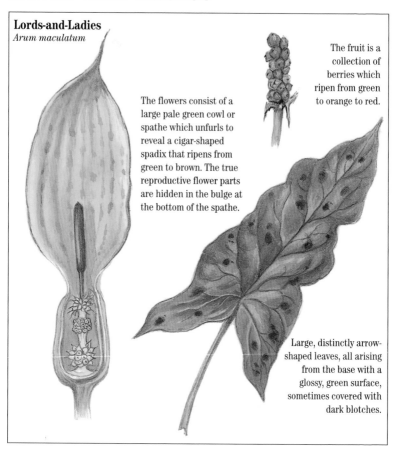

Lords-and-Ladies
Arum maculatum

The fruit is a collection of berries which ripen from green to orange to red.

The flowers consist of a large pale green cowl or spathe which unfurls to reveal a cigar-shaped spadix that ripens from green to brown. The true reproductive flower parts are hidden in the bulge at the bottom of the spathe.

Large, distinctly arrow-shaped leaves, all arising from the base with a glossy, green surface, sometimes covered with dark blotches.

Woodlands

Some of the earliest leaves to unfurl in spring are those of Lords-and-Ladies: they appear in woods and shady places under hedges and remain untouched by browsing deer or insects because they contain crystals of calcium oxylate, which feel like hundreds of tiny needles in the mouth (kidney stones, incidentally, are made of the same material). The roots were once much in demand for their starch, used for stiffening ruffs, but it caused blisters on the hands of the laundry workers. The extraordinary flowers have a remarkable property: they contain a brown, sausage-shaped spadix which can generate heat, raising the temperature a few degrees inside the cowl-like spathe (see the illustration panel, above). This, along with a faint urine-like smell, attracts flies down to the true flowers at the bottom of the cowl where they become trapped by downward-pointing hairs, sometimes overnight, so ensuring effective pollination. These flowers later go on to produce a short column of berries which ripen from green to red, lasting into early winter. The name *maculatum* means 'spotted': the leaves are sometimes dotted with dark blotches. Italian Lords-and-Ladies (*Arum italicum*), seen in southern and western Europe, has leaves with the veins clearly marked out in white, and a larger flower-head with a yellow spadix.

Lords-and-Ladies is unmistakeable: its glossy, arrow-shaped leaves are distinctive, even before the curious cigar-like flower emerges from its shroud. The green parts of the plant die off but the flowers remain to form berries in late summer, which ripen from green to orange-red.

Lords-and-Ladies

RANGE: Throughout Europe,
except the North

FLOWERING TIME
April or May

Pineappleweed/Marsh Cudweed

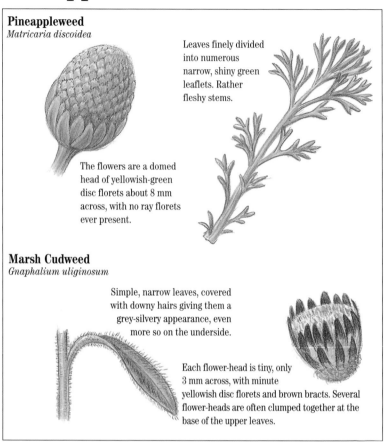

Pineappleweed
Matricaria discoidea

Leaves finely divided into numerous narrow, shiny green leaflets. Rather fleshy stems.

The flowers are a domed head of yellowish-green disc florets about 8 mm across, with no ray florets ever present.

Marsh Cudweed
Gnaphalium uliginosum

Simple, narrow leaves, covered with downy hairs giving them a grey-silvery appearance, even more so on the underside.

Each flower-head is tiny, only 3 mm across, with minute yellowish disc florets and brown bracts. Several flower-heads are often clumped together at the base of the upper leaves.

Farmland

These are both plants of pathways, often trodden on and usually ignored, but are common everywhere. **Pineappleweed** originates from northeastern Asia, but has spread around the globe, making its way into Europe chiefly in the 19th century, possibly via North America. The plant has no known use to mankind, but its favoured habitat of bare ground on paths and cultivated fields no doubt assists its spread: the seeds attach themselves to footwear. It seems to resist trampling very well, which is fortunate as this is one of the best ways to release the pineapple fragrance – a bizarre coincidence as the flower-heads resemble miniature versions of that fruit.

Marsh Cudweed is so insignificant that it often goes unnoticed, but all of us must have stepped over it at some time. It favours trodden bare ground, but only those places that get wet and muddy in winter. It does not mind if in summer its soil dries out, as the long downy hairs on the leaves (giving it a silvery appearance) help to prevent water loss. It is a member of the daisy family, and so produces flower-heads of disc florets, which are very small and are yellow for the briefest period before turning brown.

Rough wasteland

Pineappleweed *rarely reaches more than ankle-height. Its greenish-yellow 'pineapples' are a common sight on paths.*

Marsh Cudweed *is an insignificant but ubiquitous plant, the flowers too small and drab to be noticed, but the silvery-grey leaves are familiar.*

Pineappleweed

Marsh Cudweed

RANGE: Throughout Europe

RANGE: Throughout Europe, except the very far North

FLOWERING TIME
Continuously from May to November

FLOWERING TIME
July to September

Ribwort Plantain/Greater Plantain

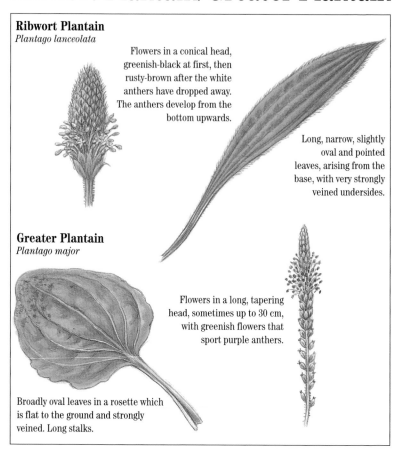

Ribwort Plantain
Plantago lanceolata

Flowers in a conical head, greenish-black at first, then rusty-brown after the white anthers have dropped away. The anthers develop from the bottom upwards.

Long, narrow, slightly oval and pointed leaves, arising from the base, with very strongly veined undersides.

Greater Plantain
Plantago major

Flowers in a long, tapering head, sometimes up to 30 cm, with greenish flowers that sport purple anthers.

Broadly oval leaves in a rosette which is flat to the ground and strongly veined. Long stalks.

Grassy meadows

Ribwort **Plantain** is a familiar plant of grassy places, whether the flower-rich meadows, the rank margins of fields or unkempt lawns. It can go unnoticed until the little satellites of white anthers develop around the rusty-brown flower-heads. The stems and leaves are extremely fibrous, and although the leaves are edible, they are tedious to prepare. They contain compounds that treat a wide range of ailments from diarrhoea to hay fever. The seeds contain a high percentage of mucilage: they swell to absorb many times their own weight in water, and this has made them useful as a laxative and for cosmetic products. The same property in the leaves has been helpful to farmers, who can judge the moisture of a haystack by feeling how dry, or otherwise, are the leaves.

Greater Plantain prefers drier spots than Ribwort Plantain, typically on the bare soil of field margins, wasteland, paths and mown lawns. Its flat leaves often get covered with dust. It has much the same medicinal properties as Ribwort Plantain, and is also widely used in medicines and cosmetics. The seeds, which are high in fibre, are also used to lower cholesterol.

Rough wasteland

224

Ribwort Plantain *leaves are easily lost among grasses and other low growth, but the ring of white anthers clearly signals their presence. Grows up to knee-height.*

Greater Plantain *is the other way round – the large flat leaves splay out over bare soil, but the dark violet anthers are almost invisible.*

Ribwort Plantain

RANGE: Throughout Europe, except the far North

FLOWERING TIME
April to October

Greater Plantain

RANGE: Throughout Europe

FLOWERING TIME
June to October

Branched Bur-reed/Bulrush

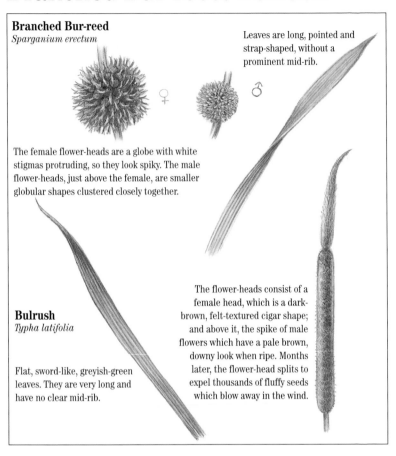

Branched Bur-reed
Sparganium erectum

Leaves are long, pointed and strap-shaped, without a prominent mid-rib.

♀ ♂

The female flower-heads are a globe with white stigmas protruding, so they look spiky. The male flower-heads, just above the female, are smaller globular shapes clustered closely together.

Bulrush
Typha latifolia

Flat, sword-like, greyish-green leaves. They are very long and have no clear mid-rib.

The flower-heads consist of a female head, which is a dark-brown, felt-textured cigar shape; and above it, the spike of male flowers which have a pale brown, downy look when ripe. Months later, the flower-head splits to expel thousands of fluffy seeds which blow away in the wind.

Both species: ponds, ditches

The edges of ponds, ditches, rivers and other watercourses are often packed with the long, thin strap-shaped leaves of various water plants. This is an adaptation to high competition for limited ground space, in a habitat that must be constantly inundated, but not too deep in standing water. Telling such plants apart by their leaves alone can only be done with experience, but fortunately the flowers are often highly distinctive. With **Branched Bur-reed** the spiky globes and knobbly balls of male and female flowers are characteristic, but you have to search for them in the jungle of leaves.

Bulrush is the giant of the pond margin: it grows easily to 2 metres or more. The large, fat brown cigar-like flowers are the female part, for the pollen is produced from the smaller spike above, though this withers away just as the female parts start to turn brown. The plant has a bewildering array of uses. The pollen may be added to flour to enhance its protein content; the young flowering spikes can be eaten raw or cooked; the base of the stem contains a starchy, nutritious centre; the roots may be boiled and eaten; the leaves may be woven into mats; and the fluffy seeds may be used as dry tinder, for stuffing mattresses and for buoyancy aids. And this leaves out an array of medicinal properties.

Branched Bur-reed *grows to waist- or chest-height in shallow water. It can only be readily distinguished by looking for the spiky balls of flowers hidden within the leaves.*

Bulrush *grows well above head-height. Even if fresh flower-heads are not in season, there are usually some old ones to aid identification.*

Branched Bur-reed

RANGE: Throughout Europe, except the far North

FLOWERING TIME
June to August

Bulrush

RANGE: Throughout Europe, except the far North

FLOWERING TIME
July to August

Mugwort/Fat Hen

Mugwort
Artemisia vulgaris

Leaves divided into pointed finger-like lobes, dark green above but silvery below with green margins, as though the leaf has been outlined.

Flowers just 3 mm across, opening yellow but soon fading to brown. The grey bracts that surround them are more noticeable.

Fat Hen
Chenopodium album

More or less diamond-shaped leaves, though much narrower at the top, with a coarsely toothed margin.

The flowers are a dense collection of tiny greenish-grey blobs, too small to be worthy of close examination.

Rough wasteland

These are both robust plants of cultivated and wasteland, and by today's standards would be regarded by most as unattractive and invasive weeds. Like so many plants, however, their history is different, and our jaundiced view of them comes from modern farmers.

Mugwort has aromatic leaves that aid digestion, especially when eaten with fatty foods, and were commonly used, like Ground-ivy (page 266), to flavour beer before hops took on that role. They were placed inside shoes to soothe sore feet; have an antibacterial effect; and can act as an insecticide. The plant is somewhat toxic, however, so should be used with caution.

Fat Hen has been found at archaeological sites of prehistoric settlements all over Europe, indicating that it has long been a useful plant. The cooked leaves make an excellent substitute for kale, but the seeds in particular provide nourishment as they contain high levels of carbohydrate and protein. They may be sprouted and eaten fresh, or ground into a flour and baked as bread. It is often the first plant to grow on recently cultivated ground, especially if the ground has been manured or well fertilized.

Farmland

Mugwort *is an erect but scruffy-looking plant of chest-height, often very dark, but with silvery undersides to the leaves which show in the breeze.*

Fat Hen *is an unprepossessing knee-high plant, with few distinguishing features save the clumps of tiny, greyish flowers.*

Mugwort

RANGE: Throughout Europe

FLOWERING TIME
June to September

Fat Hen

RANGE: Throughout Europe

FLOWERING TIME
June to October

229

Dog's Mercury/Common Nettle

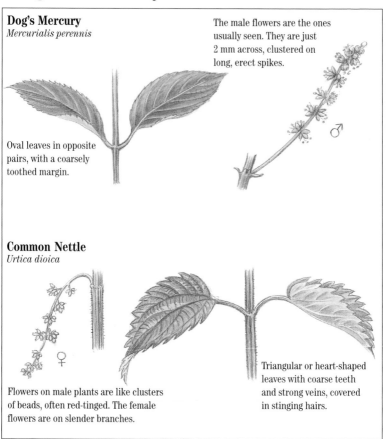

Dog's Mercury
Mercurialis perennis

The male flowers are the ones usually seen. They are just 2 mm across, clustered on long, erect spikes.

Oval leaves in opposite pairs, with a coarsely toothed margin.

♂

Common Nettle
Urtica dioica

♀

Flowers on male plants are like clusters of beads, often red-tinged. The female flowers are on slender branches.

Triangular or heart-shaped leaves with coarse teeth and strong veins, covered in stinging hairs.

Woodlands

Dog's Mercury is a member of the spurge family, and, like its cousins, the plant contains a poisonous white latex that has proved fatal to sheep. It grows in woodlands or along the bottoms of shady hedgerows on chalky soils. All its growth happens long before the tree canopy bursts into leaf and enshrouds the woodland floor in gloom. Male and female flowers are found on different plants, though the two rarely seem to grow close together, perhaps because the plant can spread easily, by means of its creeping root system, to form extensive colonies. For some reason, male colonies seem to be more common than female ones.

Common Nettle is well known to anyone who works in a country garden or walks in the countryside near farmland or wasteground: sooner or later, a leaf will brush against the skin and the stiff, hollow hairs on their surface will release a fluid that stings the skin. Many of the hairs don't sting at all, and the proportion of these varies from plant to plant. The tough stems are an excellent source of fibre; they have been used to make textiles said to be more durable than linen; and the plant also produces a green dye.

Rough wasteland

230

Dog's Mercury forms extensive carpets of green at ankle-height, without any very obvious flowers.

Common Nettle grows to chest-height, on stiff and erect stems, and particularly likes rich soil.

Dog's Mercury

RANGE: Throughout Europe, except northern Scandinavia and Ireland

FLOWERING TIME
Between February and April

Common Nettle

RANGE: Throughout Europe

FLOWERING TIME
May to September

Ivy

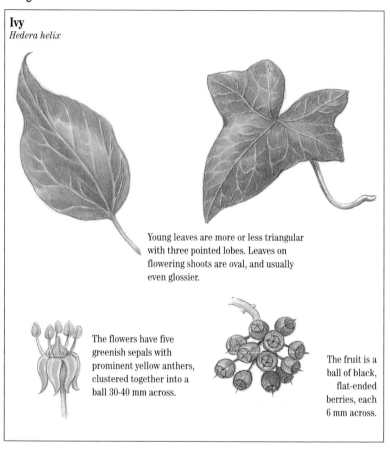

Ivy
Hedera helix

Young leaves are more or less triangular with three pointed lobes. Leaves on flowering shoots are oval, and usually even glossier.

The flowers have five greenish sepals with prominent yellow anthers, clustered together into a ball 30-40 mm across.

The fruit is a ball of black, flat-ended berries, each 6 mm across.

Woodlands

The classic ivy-leaf shape with three pointed lobes is actually only typical of young leaves – those seen climbing the bases of tree trunks, or carpeting woodlands. The leaves on the mature parts of the plant, that also give rise to the globular, greenish flower-heads, are oval and barely lobed at all. Ivy is equally at home clambering over walls and fences, but the notion that it parasitizes or damages healthy trees is false: it uses them only for support, though its weight may bring down weak limbs in time. This is one of the last plants to flower (in autumn), and sometimes produces blooms as late as November. So it is very attractive to flies and bees on warm days at that time of year, when there are few other sources of nectar. The black berries last well into the winter, and curtains of Ivy laden with fruit are important stopovers for thrushes and wood pigeons in the cold months. Traditionally, a wreath of Ivy was given to newly married couples as a symbol of fidelity. It has been used to treat whooping cough and toothache and for removing parasites, but is slightly toxic so should not be taken internally. It was also believed to nullify the effects of intoxication by alcohol. Bacchus, the Roman god of wine, wore a wreath of Ivy on his head.

Ivy leaves draped over trees and walls are familiar to everyone, but its globes of yellow-green flowers or balls of black berries are not so well known or noticed. These flowers are some of the latest to bloom in the year, providing valuable nectar for bees. It is later that the black fruits are formed.

Ivy

RANGE: Throughout Europe, except the far North

FLOWERING TIME
September to November

Curled Dock/Broad-leaved Dock

Curled Dock
Rumex crispus

Fairly narrow, rough leaves, with a distinctly wavy or 'crispy' margin.

The fruits consist of three swollen nutlets, with a rounded, untoothed membrane or 'wing'.

Broad-leaved Dock
Rumex obtusifolius

Only one of the fruit's nutlets develops and swells. It has triangular 'wings' with pointed teeth.

Much broader leaves than Curled Dock, with a heart-shaped base. They have a slightly wavy margin.

Both species: farmland

Docks are primitive plants, with whorls of simple flowers around the upper parts of their rigid stems. The flowers consist of six tiny greenish sepals around a collection of anthers and styles, only 1 or 2 mm across. It is only after the flowers have appeared, when the fruit is formed, that these clusters take on any colour: the three little nutlets may become reddish as they mature, though sometimes only one of the three develops and becomes swollen. They often have membranous 'wings' around them, sometimes with complex shapes: these are usually the clue to correct identification.

Curled Dock is a common weed of waste-places, cultivated fields and disturbed land on a variety of soils, so common that it is regarded as a serious agricultural pest. The young leaves have a pleasant, slightly acid flavour, though they are best cooked to remove the oxalic acid content, and they have long been used as a mild but effective laxative.

Broad-leaved Dock grows in exactly the same kind of locations as Curled Dock, and the two often occur and hybridize with each other. It also grows often in company with Common Nettle, and the crushed leaves applied swiftly to a nettle sting will give some slight relief from the discomfort.

Curled Dock grows slender and upright, generally at waist-height, but is very variable. It may have greenish or reddish clusters of flowers or fruit.

Broad-leaved Dock is usually a little more spreading than Curled Dock, with wide leaves flopping down.

Curled Dock

RANGE: Throughout Europe

FLOWERING TIME
June to September

Broad-leaved Dock

RANGE: Throughout Europe, except the extreme North and Iceland

FLOWERING TIME
May to October

235

Hop/Black Bryony

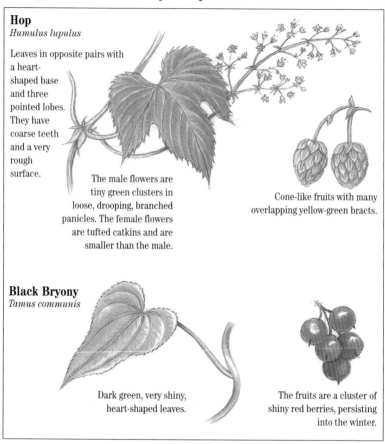

Hop
Humulus lupulus

Leaves in opposite pairs with a heart-shaped base and three pointed lobes. They have coarse teeth and a very rough surface.

The male flowers are tiny green clusters in loose, drooping, branched panicles. The female flowers are tufted catkins and are smaller than the male.

Cone-like fruits with many overlapping yellow-green bracts.

Black Bryony
Tamus communis

Dark green, very shiny, heart-shaped leaves.

The fruits are a cluster of shiny red berries, persisting into the winter.

Both species: hedgerows, roadsides

Hops are famous for their use as a flavouring for beer: its bitter fruits were first used in this way in the Netherlands in the 14th century; in Britain the hop was resisted at first in favour of traditional plants such as Ground Ivy. The plant has had a history as a food provider since Roman times, perhaps earlier: its young shoots were gathered and eaten like asparagus. Hop oil has soporific qualities, and hops are sometimes stuffed into pillows to aid sleep. In Hemp (*Cannabis sativa*) it has a close relative – but it shares none of Cannabis's well-known effects. Hop is a climbing plant which twines its way over hedgerows, along wire fences, up trees and quite often up telegraph poles.

Black Bryony is another climbing plant which works its way through hedgerows, though generally it prefers slightly shadier situations. In common with hop, the young shoots may be eaten as a kind of asparagus, though the water in which they are boiled should be changed to rinse away the slightly soapy chemical they contain. The bright red berries are extremely poisonous: and they look almost irresistible, especially in mid-winter when they persist on the dried-up vine after all other foliage has died down. This is a member of the yam family, an important source of food in the tropics.

Hop scrambles and clambers over hedges and fences. The observant may spot the characteristic leaves, but the swollen fruits in late summer are unmistakeable.

Black Bryony has leaves with an almost tropical appearance, and though the flowers are rather insignificant, the bright red berries that follow cannot be missed.

Hop

RANGE: Throughout Europe, except the far North

FLOWERING TIME
June to September

Black Bryony

RANGE: Western and southern Europe, and southern Britain

FLOWERING TIME
May to August

237

Harebell/Nettle-leaved Bellflower

Harebell
Campanula rotundifolium

Almost linear leaves. They are very thin and narrow, on equally slender stems.

The flowers are bells formed of five fused pale blue petals, in loose clusters.

The flowers are upright or horizontal bells with five pointed lobes, markedly hairy on the inside and with a prominent white stigma.

Nettle-leaved Bellflower
Campanula trachelium

Triangular leaves, sometimes with a heart-shaped base. They are hairy and have a coarsely toothed margin.

Grassy meadows

The name *Campanula* is familiar to gardeners: many varieties of bellflower have been taken from the countryside and cultivated as an attractive feature, typically of cottage gardens. The truly wild species are just as beautiful, and always a delight to discover on a country walk. The **Harebell** is the most delicate and understated of the bellflower species. Usually in short grassland, it can tolerate a wide variety of soils from the most acidic to the most alkaline, but it does not care for too much moisture, and is often found clinging to ant-hills, where the soil is particularly dry. The name *rotundifolia*, meaning round leaves, appears to be misjudged at first, but the very earliest leaves at the base of the plant are indeed rounded; dying away by flowering time.

Nettle-leaved Bellflower is a taller, stately plant, choosing semi-shaded situations alongside woods and shady hedgerows on chalky soils. Its flowers are held horizontally or even facing upwards, whereas most tall species have the bells drooping down. One exception is the Giant Bellflower (*Campanula latifolia*), which is a larger version with oval leaves, occurring throughout Europe, though chiefly in northern England.

Woodlands

Harebell's little flowers peep out of short grassland at ankle-height, the bells often swinging silently in the breeze.

Nettle-leaved Bellflower rises up proudly to knee- or waist-height, high enough above the other vegetation for its bells to be seen by all.

Harebell

RANGE: Throughout Europe, except much of Ireland

FLOWERING TIME
July to September

Nettle-leaved Bellflower

RANGE: Throughout Europe, except northern Britain and northern Scandinavia

FLOWERING TIME
July to September

Bluebell/Marsh Gentian

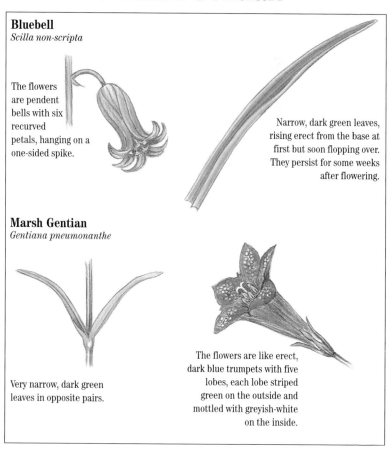

Bluebell
Scilla non-scripta

The flowers are pendent bells with six recurved petals, hanging on a one-sided spike.

Narrow, dark green leaves, rising erect from the base at first but soon flopping over. They persist for some weeks after flowering.

Marsh Gentian
Gentiana pneumonanthe

Very narrow, dark green leaves in opposite pairs.

The flowers are like erect, dark blue trumpets with five lobes, each lobe striped green on the outside and mottled with greyish-white on the inside.

Woodlands

The **Bluebell** depends on an 'Atlantic' climate: mild summers and winters with high rainfall. This is a pity as it restricts the range of one of the most delightful sights in nature. Woodlands may be completely carpeted with the drooping bell-like flowers – not to be confused with bellflowers – this is a member of the lily family. Although bluebells are found on hedge banks and coastal cliffs, the grand spring displays of millions of plants are seen in open deciduous woodland and particularly coppices. The plant is now protected in many places. The starch from the bulbs used to be used for book-binding and attaching the flights or 'fletches' to the shafts of arrows.

Marsh Gentian occurs only on the wild open and acidic conditions of bogs and wet heaths. Though the habitat alone is enough to confirm identification, it is worth examining the silver spots and greenish stripes which decorate the petals. Gentians contain a bitter principle in their roots which can be used as a digestive tonic, and the Great Yellow Gentian (*Gentiana lutea*) of Alpine regions is used commercially for that purpose, its bitter part being detectable on the tongue even when diluted to one part in 12,000.

Heathland

Bluebells are unmistakeable, with their flowers hanging gracefully from an arching stem, but even more so when seen in their millions.

Marsh Gentian flowers, only ankle-high, may remain partially hidden among the coarse grasses and rushes of bogs and heaths.

Bluebell

RANGE: Britain, Ireland, Belgium, Holland and western France

FLOWERING TIME
April to June

Marsh Gentian

RANGE: Throughout Europe, except most of Britain and Scandinavia

FLOWERING TIME
July to October

241

Field Forget-me-not/Water Forget-me-not

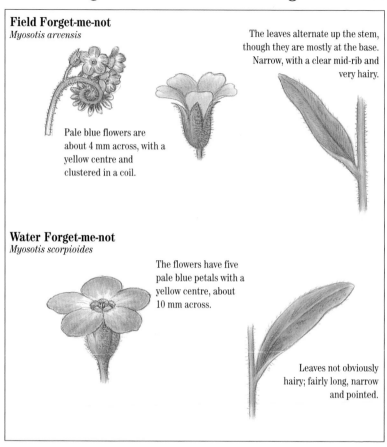

Field Forget-me-not
Myosotis arvensis

The leaves alternate up the stem, though they are mostly at the base. Narrow, with a clear mid-rib and very hairy.

Pale blue flowers are about 4 mm across, with a yellow centre and clustered in a coil.

Water Forget-me-not
Myosotis scorpioides

The flowers have five pale blue petals with a yellow centre, about 10 mm across.

Leaves not obviously hairy; fairly long, narrow and pointed.

Farmland

This delightful group of plants has the same vernacular name in most European languages. It comes from a tale in German folklore of a knight who, strolling with his lady by a river, stooped down to pick her a bunch of the pretty blooms. He stumbled and fell in, the weight of his armour pulling him down, but before he drowned he threw the flowers on to the bank crying: *"vergiss mich nicht!"* ("Forget me not!").

Field Forget-me-not is a plant of dry places, often preferring sandy soils, such as arable fields, waste-places or even alongside walls and pavements. Its small flowers and hairy leaves are characteristic, though there are several similar species. Changing Forget-me-not also has small flowers, but they open creamy-white at first, changing to yellow, then pink before finally settling for their more familiar pale blue.

Water Forget-me-not is a larger and more beautiful species than Field Forget-me-not, favouring wet marshes, ponds and stream sides. The flowers open out as a row on a curved stem called a cyme. The coil of flowers diminishes in size, resembling a scorpion's tail, which gives rise to another vernacular name for the plant.

Ponds, ditches

Field Forget-me-not
*is a modest plant,
usually not more
than ankle-high, and
easily passed by.*

Water Forget-me-not
*often forms large knee-
high colonies, its
larger flowers
complementing the
lush green foliage of
pond-side vegetation.*

Field Forget-me-not

RANGE: Throughout Europe

FLOWERING TIME
May to October

Water Forget-me-not

RANGE: Throughout Europe,
except the North

FLOWERING TIME
May to September

Germander Speedwell/Common Field Speedwell

Germander Speedwell
Veronica chamaedrys

Small leaves with coarse teeth, in opposite pairs on stems with two lines of hairs along their length.

Deep blue flowers, with three larger petals and a small white lower petal, and a white centre or 'eye', and two prominent anthers.

Common Field Speedwell
Veronica persica

Leaves a paler green than Germander Speedwell, mostly alternate on the stem, with large teeth.

The flowers have three blue petals with dark veins, one white petal with pale blue veins and two dark blue anthers.

Hedgerows, roadsides

The speedwells are delightful little plants with cheery, usually blue flowers, though there are pink and white-flowered varieties. They belong to the figwort family, which has many apparently disparate members, with such unlikely relatives as Foxglove (page 86), Mulleins and Toadflax. **Germander Speedwell** is one of the commonest and prettiest, with its vivid colour, sometimes imparting a blue mist to whole areas of grassland. The name *chamaedrys* means dwarf oak, a reference to the leaves of the plant, though they only bear the most tenuous resemblance to those of an oak tree. It is found in shady grassy areas, alongside woodland and hedgerows or on embankments.

Common Field Speedwell, on the other hand, is a plant of arable fields and other open places with bare, disturbed soil. Sometimes it occupies the gaps between rows of crops if the farmer has not used herbicides. There are several other similar species which occupy such habitats, though this one was introduced into Europe in the 19th century and has become the most prolific. It may be recognized by its flowers of three blue petals and a white lower one, which are large compared to other species.

Farmland

***Germander Speedwell's** vivid blue is punctuated with a white centre and catches the eye immediately, even when half-hidden among grass.*

***Common Field Speedwell** dislikes competition from other plants, and so is usually obvious against the bare ground of cultivated fields.*

Germander Speedwell

RANGE: Throughout Europe, except Iceland

FLOWERING TIME
April to July

Common Field Speedwell

RANGE: Throughout Europe, except the far North

FLOWERING TIME
All year round if conditions suitable

Brookline/Common Milkwort

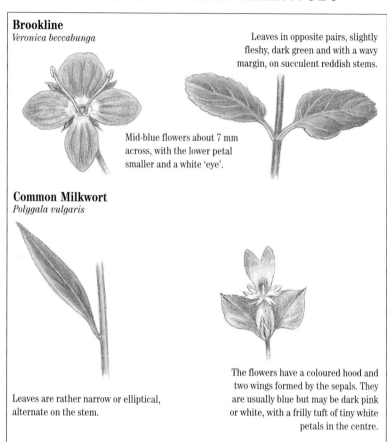

Brookline
Veronica beccabunga

Leaves in opposite pairs, slightly fleshy, dark green and with a wavy margin, on succulent reddish stems.

Mid-blue flowers about 7 mm across, with the lower petal smaller and a white 'eye'.

Common Milkwort
Polygala vulgaris

Leaves are rather narrow or elliptical, alternate on the stem.

The flowers have a coloured hood and two wings formed by the sepals. They are usually blue but may be dark pink or white, with a frilly tuft of tiny white petals in the centre.

Ponds, ditches

Brooklime is another member of the speedwell family (page 244) and its flowers are superficially similar to Germander Speedwell's. However, its succulent stems and leaves are enough to prevent confusion with any other species. It inhabits the edges of ponds and ditches or permanently wet marshes, usually where there is luxuriant growth from other plants, so it may remain hidden. One other speedwell that occupies such habitats is the Blue Water-Speedwell (*Veronica anagallis-aquatica*) which grows taller and sports its white-streaked-with-blue flowers in candle-like spikes. It also has a pink-flowered variety.

Common Milkwort is a plant of dry grassland, meadows, pastures and roadsides on chalky or limestone soils. Blue is the commonest colour of its flowers, but often they are magenta, and occasionally pure white, often growing together. The complex shape of the flowers is made up of three large coloured sepals and two tiny ones beneath, but the true petals are the white frilly structures in the centre. The plant had a reputation for increasing milk-flow in nursing mothers, but this has no scientific basis. Perhaps this was suggested to herbalists by the white petals spurting forth from the flower like milk.

Grassy meadows

Brookline *hides its flowers among the lush vegetation of pond sides. It is usually between ankle- and knee-height, but its succulent stems are sometimes more obvious than the flowers.*

__Common Milkwort__ hides its flowers among grass, also at ankle-height, but they are brighter and more eye-catching than Brookline's, though not seen until close by.

Brookline	*Common Milkwort*

RANGE: Throughout Europe, except the far North	**RANGE:** Throughout Europe, except the far North
FLOWERING TIME May to September	**FLOWERING TIME** May to September

Chicory

Chicory
Cichorium intybus

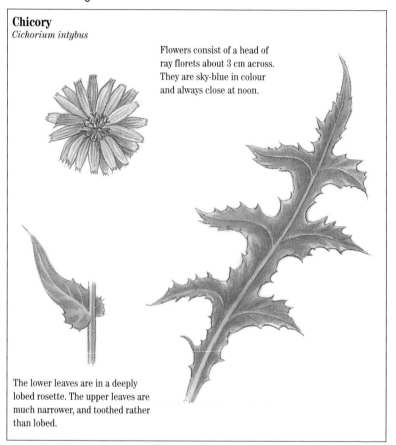

Flowers consist of a head of ray florets about 3 cm across. They are sky-blue in colour and always close at noon.

The lower leaves are in a deeply lobed rosette. The upper leaves are much narrower, and toothed rather than lobed.

Hedgerows, roadsides

Chicory flowers are the most extraordinary sky-blue: especially remarkable as it is a member of the daisy family, allied to dandelions, the flowers of which are commonly yellow or white. It is sometimes grown in gardens, particularly in one of its pink forms, but cultivated varieties are always inferior to the splendour of the natural plant. The leaves are bitter, but nonetheless a delicious ingredient in salads or as a winter vegetable if the young leaves are blanched, either by removing the lower ones and piling up earth around the stem, or by placing a pot over the plant to exclude the light. This reduces the bitterness to a palatable level. The roots also possess the bitter agent, which is the same as to be found in the roots of Dandelion, and they may be roasted and ground to make a caffeine-free substitute for coffee. More usually though, the powder is added to real coffee for the particular flavour it imparts. Chicory has a considerable history of medicinal use, especially as an aid to digestive problems, and has also been used to treat jaundice and other liver complaints. Modern research suggests that the plant may also contain agents that help to regulate the heartbeat. Chicory grows on grassy embankments and roadsides, waste-places and rough fields, usually among tall grasses on chalky soil.

Chicory's tall, almost leafless spires reach up to chest-height, sporting their pale blue flowers above the long grass. They are an unusual colour for a flower that is a member of the daisy family, whose members usually have yellow or white coloured flowers.

Chicory

RANGE: Throughout Europe,
except northern Scandinavia and much of Ireland

FLOWERING TIME
July to October

Meadow Crane's-bill/Lesser Periwinkle

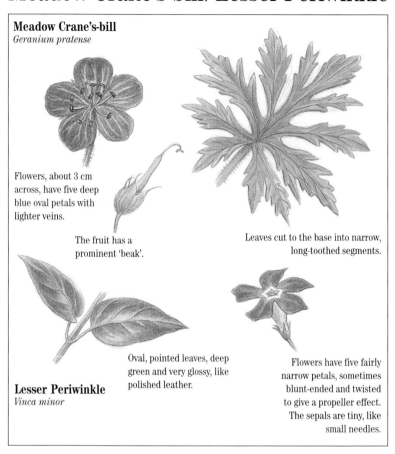

Meadow Crane's-bill
Geranium pratense

Flowers, about 3 cm across, have five deep blue oval petals with lighter veins.

The fruit has a prominent 'beak'.

Leaves cut to the base into narrow, long-toothed segments.

Oval, pointed leaves, deep green and very glossy, like polished leather.

Lesser Periwinkle
Vinca minor

Flowers have five fairly narrow petals, sometimes blunt-ended and twisted to give a propeller effect. The sepals are tiny, like small needles.

Grassy meadows

The deep violet-blue flowers of **Meadow Crane's-bill** are unusual in the geranium family, which normally sports pink flowers. It is a plant of open places such as meadows, hedge banks and particularly roadsides. The leaf-shape is the best clue to identification – see above. The characteristic beak-shaped fruit, common to all geraniums, is composed of the elongated styles of the flowers. As they dry they pull on the seeds, which are suddenly released and catapulted away from the plant.

Lesser Periwinkle produces extensive mats of evergreen leaves which carpet the ground in woods and under hedgerows. The name *Vinca* comes from the Latin *vincio* – to bind. The flowers are produced sporadically for only a few weeks, sometimes clustered together, or sometimes there may be sheets of leaves with no flower visible between them. The flowers vary in intensity of colour, and may occasionally be pure white. Greater Periwinkle (*Vinca major*), originally from southern Europe, is very similar though with slightly larger flowers and leaves, and not such a tendency to form mats. To confirm identification, examine the sepals, which are longer than the tiny ones of the smaller plant.

Woodlands

Meadow Crane's-bill's
*presence on roadsides
is signalled by its
distinctively mauve-
blue flowers nodding
above the vegetation
at knee-height.*

Lesser Periwinkle
*makes a carpet of
glossy green close
to the ground
through woods, only
displaying its flowers
for a short time.*

Meadow Crane's-bill

RANGE: Avoids Ireland, western
France and northern Scandinavia

FLOWERING TIME
June to September

Lesser Periwinkle

RANGE: Most of Europe, except the
far North and much of Ireland

FLOWERING TIME
March to May

Tufted Vetch/Common Skullcap

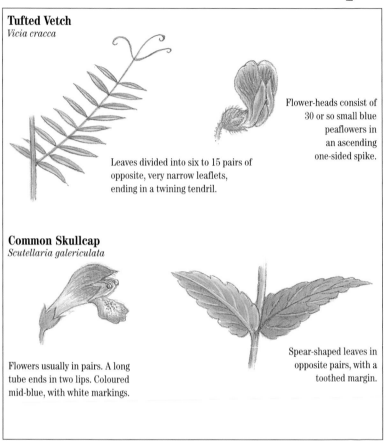

Tufted Vetch
Vicia cracca

Flower-heads consist of 30 or so small blue peaflowers in an ascending one-sided spike.

Leaves divided into six to 15 pairs of opposite, very narrow leaflets, ending in a twining tendril.

Common Skullcap
Scutellaria galericulata

Flowers usually in pairs. A long tube ends in two lips. Coloured mid-blue, with white markings.

Spear-shaped leaves in opposite pairs, with a toothed margin.

Grassy meadows

In common with other vetches, **Tufted Vetch's** leaves are adapted into tendrils: they can scramble through and twine around other vegetation in order to support themselves. This is quite an advantage: it can reach up to the light without committing resources to building a robust stem. The plant often forms considerable clumps, so large patches are coloured blue by the many flowers. It may be seen in meadows, in hedgerows, among scrub and even on coastal rocks and shingle, but rarely in pasture, for like many other members of the pea family, it makes a tasty fodder for livestock.

Common Skullcap also lacks a robust stem, and largely relies on the surrounding vegetation for support, but without any means of climbing, it has to remain in the semi-shade. Perhaps as a consequence, it produces few flowers. Their shape is thought to resemble that of a Roman leather helmet or *galerum* (hence *galericulata*). However, when in bud, they look like a tiny pair of downy boxing gloves, especially as the buds appear side by side. It grows in wet meadows and marshes, or by the margins of ponds and ditches.

Marshland

***Tufted Vetch** is seen throughout the summer, often as bushy knee-high clumps studded with violet-blue spires.*

***Common Skullcap** hides away in tall marshy vegetation, usually below knee-height, only noticed as an occasional glimpse of blue.*

Tufted Vetch

RANGE: Throughout Europe

FLOWERING TIME
June to August

Common Skullcap

RANGE: Throughout Europe, except the far North

FLOWERING TIME
June to September

Bugle/Self-heal

Bugle
Ajuga reptans

The stems are square, hairy and with a dark purple line on the corners.

The flowers are technically two-lipped, but the upper lip is greatly reduced so that the anthers project outwards. The lower lip is divided into three lobes. It is violet-blue with whitish streaks. Arranged in whorls of two to six in the leaf-axils.

Oval leaves in opposite pairs, with a slightly toothed margin. Increasingly tinged with purple towards the top of the stem. On stalks at the bottom, but stalkless higher up.

Self-heal
Prunella vulgaris

Deep blue flowers, with a hairy, hooded upper lip and smaller, three-lobed lower lip. They bloom in an irregular pattern from within the square, purple-edged calyx of sepals, each with a purple-edged bract beneath it.

Leaves in opposite pairs, often with a short stalk. They are oblong, with a purple margin, and clothed in soft hairs.

Square stems with purple edges, somewhat hairy.

Woodland

By mid-spring, the track sides and grassy clearings of deciduous woods are decked with the miniature purple-blue spires of **Bugle**. It only produces fertile seed in small quantities, but the plant makes colonies by means of long runners, which form roots and new shoots at intervals. These runners die off in the winter, but the following spring the dormant, newly-rooted plants are ready to burst into life. The Latin name *Ajuga* is a corruption of the Latin word *abigo*, meaning to drive away – a reference to the belief that it could drive away disease.

Self-heal is a related plant, held in equal high esteem for its herbal properties, and as the name suggests, was used (as an infusion) for healing wounds. It, too, spreads by means of creeping runners, but is distinguished from Bugle by the flowers which have two obvious lips, and by the close, over-lapping formation of its purple-tinged bracts and sepals. These form a tight cluster resembling a fir-cone, especially when the flowers have fallen. The plant may reach 30 cm in height, but can be as short as 5 cm in grazed lawns. Sometimes, a variety with pure pink flowers occurs, growing with the usual blue form.

Grassy meadows

Bugle *forms little spires, often purple tinged towards the tip, whose crowded little flowers are missing their upper lips.*

Self-heal *makes little pine-cone shapes of crowded purple sepals, with the flowers peeping out at irregular intervals.*

Bugle

RANGE: Europe, except Scandinavia, where Pyramidal Bugle occurs

FLOWERING TIME
Late April to June

Self-heal

RANGE: Throughout Europe

FLOWERING TIME
Almost continuously from June to October

255

Common Comfrey

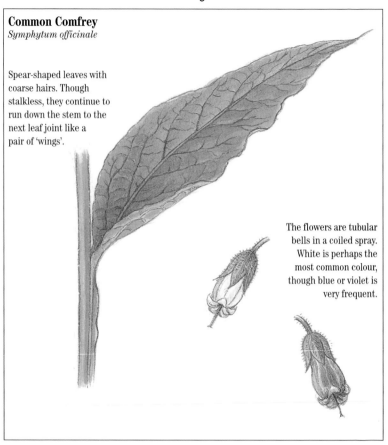

Common Comfrey
Symphytum officinale

Spear-shaped leaves with coarse hairs. Though stalkless, they continue to run down the stem to the next leaf joint like a pair of 'wings'.

The flowers are tubular bells in a coiled spray. White is perhaps the most common colour, though blue or violet is very frequent.

Ponds, ditches

Common Comfrey has been placed among the blue flowers in this guide, but it could just as easily be with the white, or the pink. Like other members of the borage family, such as the Forget-me-nots (see page 242), the flower colour is variable. In fact, Common Comfrey varies from plant to plant. The hanging, bell-shaped flowers are produced in a coiled spray, likened to a scorpion's tail, opening in sequence from the base to the tip. It grows in wet places such as river and stream margins, wet woodland and damp meadows. The plant has a long history of use for various ailments, chief of them being its apparent ability to speed the mending of broken bones. *Symphytum* comes from the Greek, *sympho* – to unite. Modern research has shown that the plant contains allantoin, a substance proven to accelerate the healing process by causing cells to multiply more quickly. It also makes an excellent manure, and, if the leaves are steeped in water, the resulting liquid feed is useful for plants that need plenty of potassium such as tomatoes. Russian Comfrey (*Symphytum x uplandicum*) is a frequently seen hybrid of Common Comfrey. It usually has blue flowers and shorter wings down the stems; it is less dependent on damp soils.

Common Comfrey is a robust plant growing waist- to chest-height. It is very leafy, but dotted with pendent bells of blue, violet, white or pink. It loves to grow in damp places but is also grown in cottage gardens for its efficacy in helping to heal wounds and mend broken bones.

Common Comfrey

RANGE: Throughout Europe, except the far North

FLOWERING TIME
May to July

Viper's-bugloss/Sea Holly

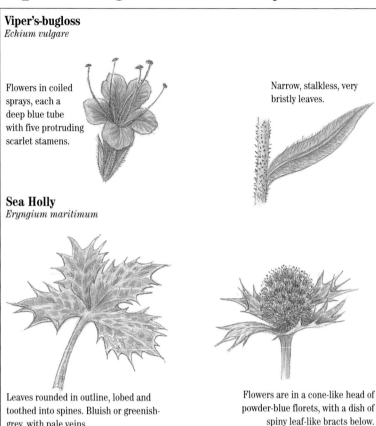

Viper's-bugloss
Echium vulgare

Flowers in coiled sprays, each a deep blue tube with five protruding scarlet stamens.

Narrow, stalkless, very bristly leaves.

Sea Holly
Eryngium maritimum

Leaves rounded in outline, lobed and toothed into spines. Bluish or greenish-grey, with pale veins.

Flowers are in a cone-like head of powder-blue florets, with a dish of spiny leaf-like bracts below.

Grassy meadows

Viper's-bugloss occurs in dry open habitats, such as road verges, grassy banks, sand dunes and coastal shingle, on all but the most acid soils. The name *Echium* comes from *echis*, meaning a snake. Several explanations have been given for this, all somewhat fanciful. The seeds supposedly resemble a snake's head; the spotting of the stems a snake's skin; and the protruding red stamens what else but the flickering tongue of a serpent. All this was taken by early herbalists to signify that the plant was a cure for snake bite, or indeed a scorpion's sting, the coil of flowers being curved like a scorpion's tail.

Sea Holly belongs to a group of plants which have become popular in gardens for their architectural appearance and misty blue flowers. It occurs solely on sandy beaches, a habitat not normally associated with grazing animals, and in which the plant's very effective armour of fierce spines would seem unnecessary. The leaves have a tough texture, something like dried leather, which means they can retain moisture when fresh water is scarce. At one time, the roots were dug up and candied to make sweets, thought particularly good as a cough remedy. This almost wiped out the plant, and it remains a rarity.

Coast

Viper's-bugloss produces unmistakeable purple-blue spires of flowers reaching waist-height.

Sea Holly is just as distinctive as Viper's-bugloss. The spikiness of the grey-blue leaves can almost be felt without touching.

Viper's-bugloss

RANGE: Most of Europe, except the far North and Ireland

FLOWERING TIME
June to September

Sea Holly

RANGE: On coasts throughout Europe, except the far North

FLOWERING TIME
June to September

259

Teasel

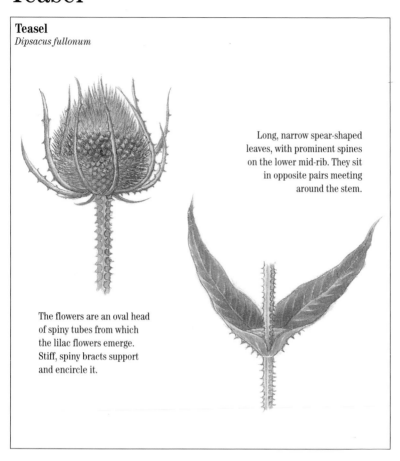

Teasel
Dipsacus fullonum

Long, narrow spear-shaped leaves, with prominent spines on the lower mid-rib. They sit in opposite pairs meeting around the stem.

The flowers are an oval head of spiny tubes from which the lilac flowers emerge. Stiff, spiny bracts support and encircle it.

Hedgerows, roadsides

There are many unusual features about this plant. One is the succession followed by the opening flowers. They start in a concentric ring about half of the way up the flower-head, then the ring splits and advances both up and down the head simultaneously. The flower-head is extremely spiny, and the dried heads were used in the wool industry for carding or teasing out the wool strands. A related variety has spines which are recurved or hooked, at the tip, and these are still used today for raising the knap on specialist cloths. The spines have exactly the right amount of springiness for the job, without catching and tearing the fabric, a facility which cannot be reproduced by steel or any other artificial material. Another unusual feature is the spiny-veined leaves. Though in opposite pairs, they are joined to each other around the stem with a membrane, so that in large specimens a considerable amount of rainwater and dew collects in them. This invariably contains drowned insects, but such water was thought to possess magical properties, such as removing unwanted freckles. The name *Dipsacus* refers to this water retention, being derived from the Greek for thirst. Teasel occurs in rough grassy places along embankments and roadsides; also beside hedgerows and woodland.

Teasel's flower-heads rise up to head-height above the rank grasses of roadsides like spiny, jewel-encrusted sceptres. Lilac-blue flowers emerge between the dense collection of stiff, straight spines. The leaves are also unmistakeable, with their bold white mid-rib armed with long prickles underneath.

Teasel

RANGE: Much of Europe except Denmark, Scandinavia and large parts of Ireland

FLOWERING TIME
July to September

Field Scabious/Devil's-bit Scabious

Field Scabious
Knautia arvensis

The leaves, in opposite pairs, are deeply divided into narrow opposite segments.

The flowers are a flat head of pinkish-lilac tubular florets, with larger florets on the outside.

Devil's-bit Scabious
Succisa pratensis

Leaves at the base are lance-shaped with a pale mid-rib. Upper leaves are in opposite pairs and toothed.

Flowers are a rounded head of florets all the same size, with protruding stamens. Heads in bud look like a ball of beads.

Both these plants belong to the same family as the Teasel (page 260), and although they look different to that plant, they both have flowers with tubular petals.

Field Scabious produces a flat head of tubular florets flattened out
Hedgerows, roadsides at the end, in many ways similar to those of a dandelion, whose petals are, however, flat. So the two families are in fact quite closely related. The plant was originally called *Scabiosa arvensis*, because the juice of the roots was used to treat scabies and other skin disorders. It was later named after the 17th century German botanist, Dr. Knaut. It grows in grassy meadows, pastures and roadside verges on chalky soils.

Devil's-bit Scabious tolerates a wider variety of soils than Field Scabious, and may be found on dry or damp pastures, meadows and heaths. In its first year of growth, it develops a long tap root, similar to a carrot swollen at the base. Later, the lower part of this withers and dies, leaving an abruptly ended stump, whilst further side roots develop. According to legend, the Devil came up from Hell and bit off the root because he wanted to kill the plant out of envy for the good that it might do mankind. It has many medicinal uses.

Grassy meadows

262

Field Scabious tends to be tall, producing its flat-topped lilac-blue flowers at least waist-high.

Devil's-bit Scabious is usually shorter, producing rounded purple-blue flowers closer to knee-height, sometimes in great abundance.

Field Scabious

RANGE: Throughout Europe, except the extreme North

FLOWERING TIME
July to September

Devil's-bit Scabious

RANGE: Throughout Europe, except the extreme North

FLOWERING TIME
July to October

Bush Vetch/Ivy-leaved Toadflax

Bush Vetch
Vicia sepium

Leaves divided into five to nine pairs of opposite, oval leaflets with a long tendril at the end.

Flowers are typically pea-shaped. Bluish or purplish, with darker veins, turning pale brown quickly. A cluster of flowers is usually multi-coloured.

Ivy-leaved Toadflax
Cymbalaria muralis

Flowers, about 12 mm long, have pale violet upper and lower lips with pale yellow bosses or 'palates' in the centre.

The leaves are like tiny Ivy leaves with three or five pointed lobes, usually yellowish-green.

Woodlands

It is difficult to pin down the colour of **Bush Vetch** flowers. They are more or less mauve, or lilac, or purple, but often all three with veins of one colour over another. They may also be a steely grey-blue, especially as they mature. Once they have been pollinated however, they quickly turn a pale brown colour, hence the name *sepium* from *sepia* – a reddish-brown. They do this even though the petals are still fresh. It is probably a mechanism to prevent insects trying to get nectar from these flowers: from the plant's point of view this is wasted effort and would be better employed visiting unpollinated blooms. The plant is found in shaded situations such as hedgerows and woodlands, avoiding acid soils.

Ivy-leaved Toadflax is much associated with man: it rarely occurs in completely wild situations, and is frequently seen on old walls, particularly of churches or ruins (*muralis* means 'of walls'). It is a native of the mountain ranges of Italy and Switzerland, but has since been introduced to other parts of Europe. Its seed-heads bend away from the light when mature, towards the rock or wall face. In this way the seeds may be more likely to fall into a crevice and germinate.

Rough wasteland

Bush Vetch *scrambles and clambers through grasses and other undergrowth. It has understated flowers, usually attaining no more than knee-height.*

Ivy-leaved Toadflax *clambers over walls, its diminutive but cheerful little flowers peeping out from a tight mat of leaves.*

Bush Vetch

RANGE: Throughout Europe, except the extreme North

FLOWERING TIME
May to October

Ivy-leaved Toadflax

RANGE: Western Europe and southern Scandinavia

FLOWERING TIME
May to September

Ground-ivy

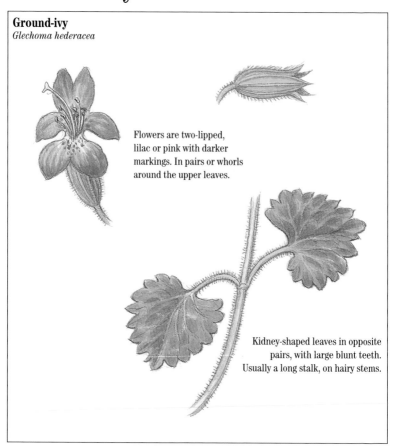

Ground-ivy
Glechoma hederacea

Flowers are two-lipped,
lilac or pink with darker
markings. In pairs or whorls
around the upper leaves.

Kidney-shaped leaves in opposite
pairs, with large blunt teeth.
Usually a long stalk, on hairy stems.

Hedgerows, roadsides

Ground-ivy cannot always decide what shade its flowers should be: they range between mauve, lilac, blue or even pink. But there is something about the colour that always makes it instantly recognizable. It flowers all summer long, but its big show is in early spring, when there may be extensive mats of flowers carpeting the ground like mist. It prefers bare ground, provided it is a little damp: typical locations are field margins, bare patches in meadows, or even the shade of woodlands or hedgerows. The name *hederacea* means resembling Ivy, which it does in two ways: it sends out long runners over the ground (which form roots at intervals); and it remains green throughout the winter. The plant was the chief flavouring and clearing ingredient in beer before hops became widely used for that purpose in the 16th century. It has also had many medicinal uses such as treating problems of the mucous membranes, and dealing with catarrh. Sometimes small furry round balls the size of a pea may be seen attached to the plant. These 'galls' are caused by a tiny wasp, *Liposthenes glechomae*, laying an egg in the stem of the plant, which responds by growing tissue around the egg. The egg hatches and the larva develops inside the gall, over-wintering there, until it hatches as an adult wasp.

Ground-ivy forms carpets of mauve to pinkish flowers, usually close to the ground, though sometimes reaching to above ankle-height. Although it may flower throughout the summer, it is in early spring that its extensive mats bloom. Like Ivy, it spreads by sending long, leafy runners over the ground.

Ground-ivy

RANGE: Throughout Europe, except the far North

FLOWERING TIME
March to September, but mostly Spring

267

Sea Aster/Sea-lavender

Sea Aster
Aster tripolium

The leaves are almost linear, and rounded in cross-section. They are arranged alternately up the stem. Rather succulent.

The flower-heads are a small collection of bright yellow disc florets, surrounded by a few mauve or lilac ray florets, though sometimes the ray florets are missing

Sea-lavender
Limonium vulgare

Long, narrow leaves, all collected at the base. They have a single vein and a long stalk.

Flat-topped flower-heads with numerous tubular lilac flowers. Each is surrounded by a papery bract, like those of the (related) Thrift (see page 96).

Coast

Most gardeners are familiar with the Michaelmas Daisy (a member of the Aster family) which originates from North America and is such a popular choice to add late summer colour to flower beds. The **Sea Aster** is the European native cousin to those plants, often waiting until September before opening its blooms to enliven the mud of saltmarshes and estuaries. At high tide it may even be completely inundated, but it can withstand the harsh, salty conditions by storing fresh water in its succulent stems. Usually the flowers have a centre of yellow disc florets surrounded by mauve ray florets, but sometimes a form occurs with the rays missing so that only the yellow disc is in view, giving the plant a quite different look. In some areas this form is becoming commoner.

Sea-lavender lives in similar conditions, surviving regular flooding by sea water. It is somewhat variable in height, growing tall in the drier parts of the marsh. Salt water renders the seeds of most plants useless, but in Sea-lavender the action of salt appears to increase the likelihood of seed germination, though they will not germinate in sea water itself. Instead, sufficient rainfall must occur to surround the seed in fresh water, when successful germination will take place.

Sea Aster grows to knee-height, though this is only evident at low tide. It forms stands of lilac and yellow daisies in the mud of saltmarshes.

Sea-lavender grows a little shorter than Sea Aster, and usually creates extensive swathes of colour across the mud in midsummer.

Sea Aster

RANGE: European coasts

FLOWERING TIME
July to October

Sea-lavender

RANGE: European coasts, except the far North and western Britain

FLOWERING TIME
July to September

Bittersweet

Bittersweet
Solanum dulcamara

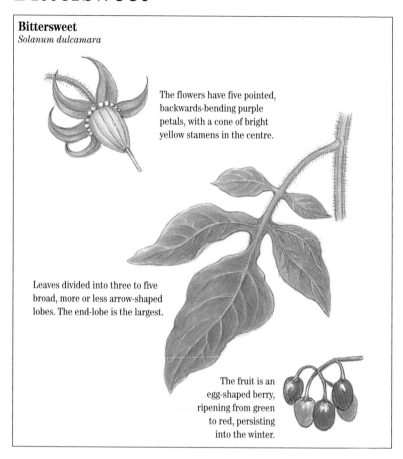

The flowers have five pointed, backwards-bending purple petals, with a cone of bright yellow stamens in the centre.

Leaves divided into three to five broad, more or less arrow-shaped lobes. The end-lobe is the largest.

The fruit is an egg-shaped berry, ripening from green to red, persisting into the winter.

Hedgerows, roadsides

Bittersweet grows in a wide variety of situations. It climbs chiefly over hedges and scrub and shaded places, but may also be found twining its way around reeds in wet reed-beds. When it grows in a reed-bed along with Common Nettle and Greater Willowherb, this is a sign that the swamp is beginning to dry out. There is even a variety that grows on coastal shingle, where in the absence of a climbing frame, it sprawls over a wide area.

This is a member of the potato family, and the flowers are a miniature version of potato flowers, or of the all-yellow flowered tomato. The family also includes such infamous plants as Deadly Nightshade (*Atropa belladonna*), and Henbane (*Hyoscyamus niger*), both of which are deadly poisonous. Whilst Bittersweet is far from deadly, it should certainly be treated as poisonous, though it has in the past been used for treating various conditions including skin eruptions and warts.

The name *dulcamara* means sweet and bitter: supposedly the chewed roots taste bitter at first, then sweet. The berries look particularly appealing, changing colour as they ripen from green to orange to brilliant scarlet. They remain in place until winter, hanging in clusters like painted eggs from the bare woody stems: avoid nonetheless.

Bittersweet's purple and yellow flowers droop down from the greenery of its climbing stems, but the bright red fruits are even more obvious. These fruits persist long after the leaves have withered. In common with other members of the potato family, the entire plant is poisonous.

Bittersweet

RANGE: Throughout Europe, except the far North

FLOWERING TIME
May to September

Marsh Cinquefoil/Honesty

Marsh Cinquefoil
Potentilla palustris

Leaves divided into five finger-like lobes with a serrated margin, on long stalks. Upper leaves may be single-lobed.

The flowers have five triangular maroon sepals, with small narrow red petals between them, and a dome of female ovaries resembling a strawberry, in loose clusters.

Honesty
Lunaria annua

Flowers have four, oval purple petals, though white forms occur quite commonly.

Distinctly heart-shaped leaves, with coarse, jagged teeth on the margin.

The fruit is a circular disc, 3 cm across, at first green, then transparent. It splits to leave a single, thin membrane with the seeds attached.

Marshland

Marsh Cinquefoil belongs to the rose family, and is allied to the group of *Potentillas* which has five distinct lobes to the leaf. In this case, they radiate out like the fingers of a hand. It lives in marshes, wet meadows and bogs, favouring places where the water table has just dipped below the surface of the ground during the summer. It generally prefers rather acid soils. The true petals of the flower are tiny red strips, but the sepals do the work of advertising the plant's presence with an unusual maroon colour: the flower looks as though it were made of paper or card. In common with many other plants of this colour it is usually pollinated by flies and wasps.

Honesty was introduced to Europe from Italy in the 16th century, as a cheerful garden plant. Its merits include not only its four large purple petals (indicating that it is a member of the cabbage family), but also the thin, membranous fruits which are used in dried flower arrangements. These are green at first but dry out to become transparent, so the seeds may be seen. Eventually they become round, silvery discs looking like the moon: hence the name *Lunaria*. It is an annual and self-seeds in the countryside at large.

Hedgerows, roadsides

Marsh Cinquefoil's *extraordinary maroon sepals and 'strawberry' flowers often remain hidden at knee-height among long rushes and grasses.*

Honesty *is a bold plant of spring, its purple flowers singing out at knee-height from the hedgerows.*

Marsh Cinquefoil

RANGE: Throughout Europe, though less common in western France

FLOWERING TIME
May to July

Honesty

RANGE: Throughout Europe, except most of Scandinavia

FLOWERING TIME
April to June

Sweet Violet/Common Dog-violet

Sweet Violet
Viola odorata

The flowers have five violet or purple petals, white in the centre, with dark purple lines, and a pouch or spur at the back which is also purple. Sometimes white flowers with a pink spur occur.

Leaves in basal tufts, with a fairly rounded or kidney-shaped outline, and a bluntly-toothed edge.

Common Dog-violet
Viola riviniana

Leaves are smaller and more pointed or heart-shaped than Sweet Violet's.

The flowers are a paler shade of violet than Sweet Violet's. The spur is also much paler and it is slightly grooved at the tip.

Hedgerows, roadsides

There are many species of violet, often difficult to separate, but these two are perhaps the most widely distributed. The first clue to identifying **Sweet Violet** is its flowering time, which may be as early as February. Purple (very occasionally white) flowers peer through the rounded leaves and continue to multiply throughout the summer. The flower has a sweet scent and has been cultivated not only for cut flowers but also for making a syrup by boiling them up with sugar, used in confectionary. The springtime flowers only rarely set seed, as there are few pollinating insects at that time. A second crop of special flowers are produced in the autumn. These have no petals, and do not open fully. The plant self-fertilizes, and can produce seed, although it also spreads by creeping stems. It can be found in semi-shaded spots alongside woods, hedgerows and paths.

Common Dog-violet is a similar, though scentless, plant usually found deeper within woodlands, and which flowers later, though still before the trees come into leaf. The leaves of this and other violets are an important food for caterpillars of certain butterflies, especially the Fritillaries, as the leaves persist for months after the flowers have faded.

Woodlands

Sweet Violet *is one of the first of the shade-loving plants to appear in spring, the flowers looming above leaves on the ground.*

Common Dog-violet *is more likely than Sweet Violet to be seen in association with other woodland wild flowers such as primrose or wood anemone.*

Sweet Violet

RANGE: Throughout Europe, except the far North

FLOWERING TIME
February to May

Common Dog-violet

RANGE: Throughout Europe, except the extreme North

FLOWERING TIME
April to June

Hedge Woundwort

Hedge Woundwort
Stachys sylvatica

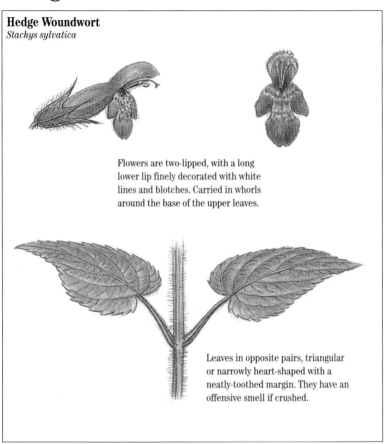

Flowers are two-lipped, with a long lower lip finely decorated with white lines and blotches. Carried in whorls around the base of the upper leaves.

Leaves in opposite pairs, triangular or narrowly heart-shaped with a neatly-toothed margin. They have an offensive smell if crushed.

Hedgerows, roadsides

Hedge Woundwort is allied to the mint family, and like all those plants it has stems which are square in cross-section, and leaves which are in opposite pairs, each pair at right-angles and therefore on different sides of the square than the preceding pair. When the petals of the flower fade and fall out, four tiny developing nutlets can be seen within the spiky tube made by the fused sepals. This is a plant of woodland edges and hedgerows, preferring places that afford it some shade during the day. This is often true of dark-flowered plants, and they often have an unpleasant or foetid smell, that can be easily experienced by crushing the leaves. This, and other *Stachys* species, are said to be effective for staunching bleeding wounds if applied fresh to the affected area.

Downy Woundwort (*Stachys germanica*) is even more effective as a dressing, as its leaves are covered with thick white hairs like felt to give it a degree of absorbancy. It is also reputed to yield a yellow dye.

Marsh Woundwort (*Stachys palustris*) is a similar plant of wet places by ponds and ditches, but in more open situations. It is a very attractive plant, with densely-packed heads of pink flowers.

Hedge Woundwort is a rather cheery waist-high plant of neat appearance, in spite of its dark-coloured flowers and its tendency to skulk in the shadows. Although the dark purple flowers do not seem bright enough to attract insects, the petals do have white markings on them which guide bees and flies to the throat of the flower to help pollination. The strong, foetid smell of the leaves may also attract insects.

Hedge Woundwort

RANGE: Throughout Europe,
except the extreme North

FLOWERING TIME
June to September

Hound's-tongue/Common Figwort

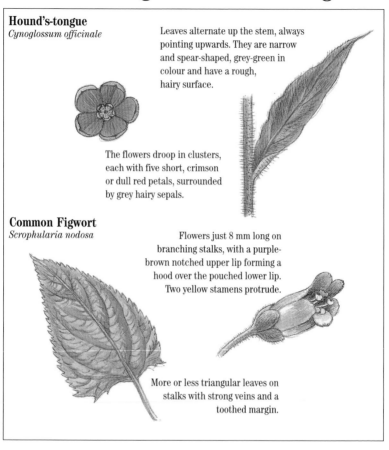

Hound's-tongue
Cynoglossum officinale

Leaves alternate up the stem, always pointing upwards. They are narrow and spear-shaped, grey-green in colour and have a rough, hairy surface.

The flowers droop in clusters, each with five short, crimson or dull red petals, surrounded by grey hairy sepals.

Common Figwort
Scrophularia nodosa

Flowers just 8 mm long on branching stalks, with a purple-brown notched upper lip forming a hood over the pouched lower lip. Two yellow stamens protrude.

More or less triangular leaves on stalks with strong veins and a toothed margin.

Grassy meadows

Hound's-tongue is a coarse and hairy plant of rough grassland, often found close to scrub or hedgerows on chalky soils. It is a member of the borage family (like the Forget-me-nots), and like them the clusters of flowers uncoil from curved branches as they open. The deep crimson flowers have a distinctive and somewhat unpleasant smell of mouse urine. Once pollinated, they go on to produce four large nutlets, which are green and covered with small bristles, tightly packed together into the remains of the sepals, looking like four miniature tennis balls in a box. The name *Cynoglossum* means dog-tongue, in reference to the rough surface of the leaves.

Common Figwort likes damp places, favouring rich soil and some shade: it is found alongside woodlands or river banks with overhanging trees. The flowers seem too small for the plant, arranged at the ends of thin splayed-out branches like beads, and are pollinated by small wasps attracted by their faint, malodorous smell. The plant has long been used as a treatment for skin problems such as small wounds, boils and scrophula, from which it gets its Latin name. *Nodosa* refers to the roots, which bear swollen nodules.

Woodlands

Hound's-tongue's *rough grey leaves arch outwards like a knee-high dry fountain spraying small crimson blooms.*

Common Figwort *is a secretive plant which keeps to the shadows bearing the most insignificant of flowers in a branched candelabra at waist-height.*

Hound's-tongue

RANGE: Throughout Europe, except northern Scandinavia and Ireland

FLOWERING TIME
May to August

Common Figwort

RANGE: Throughout Europe, except the extreme North

FLOWERING TIME
June to September

279

Purple Loosestrife

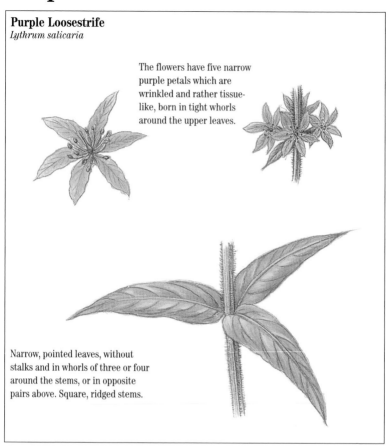

Purple Loosestrife
Lythrum salicaria

The flowers have five narrow purple petals which are wrinkled and rather tissue-like, born in tight whorls around the upper leaves.

Narrow, pointed leaves, without stalks and in whorls of three or four around the stems, or in opposite pairs above. Square, ridged stems.

Marshland

Purple Loosestrife brings cheer to marshes, fens, wet meadows and the margins of ponds, rivers and ditches. It has been proved effective against stomach disorders, even for babies, and is a natural antibiotic that may even be useful in treating typhus. Its tall, pinkish-purple spires are regarded as beautiful by most, though in some countries this is not the case. Just as some plants introduced into Europe from other continents cause problems because they are so invasive (for example, Japanese Knotweed and Himalayan Balsam), so it is with Purple Loosestrife outside Europe. In much of the United States, Canada and New Zealand this plant is listed as a pest, spreading rapidly and widely to the detriment of native plants. This tends to happen when a single species of plant moves from one place to another without the insects, fungi, viruses and other components of an ecosystem that normally keep it in a healthy balance with its environment. It is sad that plants are still introduced to unsuitable places without a thought about the monsters they may become. New Zealand Pigmyweed (*Crassula helmsii*) and Floating Pennywort (*Hydrocotyle ranunculoides*) are being sold as garden plants in Europe, and yet they are threatening to make extinct some of our rarest native plants, having taken over their habitats.

Purple Loosestrife is easily recognized by its tall candelabras of numerous purple flowers at chest-height, making this plant unmissable in wet meadows and marshes. Although attractive, it can quickly become a pest as it colonizes large areas to the detriment of native species. Purple Loosestrife often grows with the unrelated Yellow Loosestrife.

Purple Loosestrife

RANGE: Throughout Europe,
except the far North

FLOWERING TIME
June to August

INDEX

Index